FUN in the FIELD

A Wiltshire Farmer's Sporting Life

Barry Wookey

© Copyright 2006 Barry Wookey.
All rights reserved. No part of this publication may be reproduced, stored in a retrieval system, or transmitted, in any form or by any means, electronic, mechanical, photocopying, recording, or otherwise, without the written prior permission of the author.

Note for Librarians: A cataloguing record for this book is available from Library and Archives Canada at www.collectionscanada.ca/amicus/index-e.html
ISBN 1-4120-8599-3

Printed in Victoria, BC, Canada. Printed on paper with minimum 30% recycled fibre. Trafford's print shop runs on "green energy" from solar, wind and other environmentally-friendly power sources.

Offices in Canada, USA, Ireland and UK

Book sales for North America and international:
Trafford Publishing, 6E–2333 Government St.,
Victoria, BC V8T 4P4 CANADA
phone 250 383 6864 (toll-free 1 888 232 4444)
fax 250 383 6804; email to orders@trafford.com
Book sales in Europe:
Trafford Publishing (UK) Limited, 9 Park End Street, 2nd Floor
Oxford, UK OX1 1HH UNITED KINGDOM
phone 44 (0)1865 722 113 (local rate 0845 230 9601)
facsimile 44 (0)1865 722 868; info.uk@trafford.com
Order online at:
trafford.com/06-0355

10 9 8 7 6 5 4 3 2

To

The Future of Country Field Sports

Long may they continue

FOREWORD

I was lucky enough to have been brought up on a large farm in Wiltshire, situated between the Vale of Pewsey and Salisbury Plain. The western boundary is formed by the River Avon and the eastern boundary is on the high downs. This being the case it is not surprising, therefore, that we grew up to accept hunting, shooting and fishing as part of our lives. As children we all had ponies, the .410 was a prized possession of boys and with a river at the bottom of the garden, the fish had little peace in the summer holidays.

Now approaching the age when it is considered wise to cut down on some of our former activities, fishing is the only field sport left, the guns having been sold and horses, at least for me to ride, are a no-go area according to my wife! But I have always kept records and/or diaries to remind me in my later years of the fun we used to enjoy, whether hunting, shooting or fishing. I always said I would one day collate the various note books, game books, fishing records, etc. to illustrate how things used to be, primarily, to be honest, for my own enjoyment but to do it in book form in case anyone was ever interested in publishing it.

I pondered for a long time on how to set the book out - whether by subject or in chronological order of events and have finally decided to do it as the events took place. This means that all the sports are mixed up but that is how our forbears ordained rural pursuits. Starting at Michaelmas, the traditional start of the farming year, shooting is first up. Grouse shooting (although not in Wiltshire) starts on the 12th August, partridges on the 1st of September and pheasants on the 1st of October. The opening meet of the local foxhounds is on or near the 1st of November and the hunting season lasts until March or April (not many hunts try and kill a May fox as they used to) by which time fishing is upon us. Salmon fishing on the Avon (Wiltshire) starts about mid-March (although there are no salmon about nowadays until May or thereabouts) and trout fishing starts on April 15th. From this you can see that the all-round field sportsman can enjoy his sports throughout the year and this I have endeavoured to convey in the following pages.

CONTENTS

Foreword
Chapter 1.   India 1945-48.   Shooting. Partition.
Chapter 2.   Demob.1948-55.   Hunting. Marriage. Norway.
Chapter 3.   1953-1959.   Shooting. The Parker era.
Chapter 4.   7 Oct. 1960.   Record Partridge Day.
Chapter 5.   Salmon and Trout.   Joe Maggs. A.G.Street. Testwood

Chapter 6.   Triathlon.
Chapter 7.   Norway.   Salmon fishing. Kaare (the ghillie)

Chapter 8.   Roger's pike.
Chapter 9.   Horses and Hunting. Boxing Days. Horse Sales. Rushall One Day Event

Chapter 10. Changes in shooting.
Chapter 11. Etna and the Shin.   Norway and Scotland.
Chapter 12. Game Fair 1979.   The Gun Dog Section.
Chapter 13. Gerry's pike.
Chapter 14. Plantagenet.   The star Rushall horse – Written by Jane

Chapter 15. Odds and ends.

Appendices
A   Why we adopted Organic Farming.
B   Nest and Hatch records - Upavon and Littlecott 1954.
C   'Old Boy News' - News from purchasers of horses sold.
D   Sayings, etc. noted over the years.

Chapter 1

INDIA 1945/48

Gateway to India

After VE Day, May 1945, all the newly commissioned Royal Engineer subalterns were sent to India to join the Royal Indian Engineers and because VJ Day arrived soon after, we were left in India until our "demob" number came up. Mine was 59 so I had to wait until 1948 to be repatriated and "demobbed". We were therefore in India during the Partition and the terrible carnage caused by that decision.

India 1945/1948

Our main field sport in India was shooting. I had taken my 12 bore with me and on the advice of our old Scottish keeper I had sealed up both ends of the barrels with candle wax to prevent corrosion by the sea air - we went to Bombay by sea via the newly opened Suez Canal. Whether it did any good or not I don't know - what I do know was it was a terrible job to clean it all up!

Threshing bajra with bullocks

As very junior subalterns our shooting was rather limited. We would hire a "shikari" - a shooting guide - to take us out to shoot whatever was available. Mostly we went after a sort of jungle fowl or peacock. We would go out in hired Army 15 cwt. trucks to a village where the shikari would negotiate for some beaters and we would have various drives out of sugar cane. Sometimes the birds flew, more often they ran but occasionally we would shoot one - quite an excitement for all concerned. Then we would try for peacock out of "nullahs" - dry river beds. We would stand in the bottom and the peacock would be driven over us and I clearly remember that I never shot one! They seemed huge with their long tails - rather like a jumbo jet flying low overhead - and I never could hit one! I often wondered if they somehow lived charmed lives as they were sacred to some castes of Indians and occasionally the "gaon wallahs" - villagers - would get a bit cross and we had to move out.

The highlight of our shooting in India would be when we were invited by the Colonel to join his duck shoot. This was a major operation with a Mess Tent staffed by a full complement of servants. A convoy of bullock carts would set forth from the barracks, tents would be pitched at the camp site near the jheels (lakes) ready for the arrival of the Colonel and us lesser mortals. With hind-sight, I think we, the subalterns, were only included as glorified beaters as, when operations started, the Colonel and his friends would be dispatched to the central jheels while we were posted on the outlying ones to help keep the duck on the move. Nevertheless, it was a wonderful opportunity and we thoroughly enjoyed it. The evening flight saw us in a boat on the way to a hide amongst the reeds where we stayed till dark. We were then escorted back to the camp for a full-blown dinner after the bag had been counted. Then up early for the morning flight to be followed by breakfast, after which we left for home.

I cannot remember all the varieties of duck that were shot but the one variety I always wanted to shoot - and failed miserably - was a pintail. Looking back, I think it must have been the same as with peacock - too much tail caused me to shoot too far back.

India 1945/1948

Another little matter that doesn't affect wildfowlers in England is the necessity to eviscerate the duck as soon as possible after shooting. Although the evening and morning flights were conducted in comparatively cool temperatures, the days become very hot with obvious problems!

Local transport for shooting

We would also go after black buck with our shikari and again I have the feeling that we were used as accessories because of all the buck shot - very few - all were shot by the shikari! We would use solid bullets in our shotguns so the range was not very great but we never got one.

One day we were walking back to our truck when the shikari saw a flock of starlings in a dead tree. He quickly loaded with very small shot and blasted at the thickest patch of the birds and felled about 30. He immediately dropped his gun, whipped out his knife and proceeded to cut the throats of all the birds. Being

India 1945/1948

a Muslim, he could only eat, or sell, birds that had been killed by having their throats cut - halal - but how he managed to convince his family or friends that he had killed them by cutting their throats I never did discover.

My fishing in India was non-existent but with hindsight I think I missed a great opportunity. The Ganges Canal ran through Roorkee - and still does I suppose - and we used it for training. It was too wide for a clear span bridge so we practised building floating bridges. These are bridges built onto pontoons anchored in the water which, in spite of making you feel sea-sick when driving across them as they rise and fall as the weight comes onto each pontoon, they were very effective. But to the fishing - the canal had a current as it carried water from the Ganges to the U.P. and contained a lot of mahseer. I have never caught one but from reading about them it seems I could have had a lot of fun. What a pity!

I cannot move on to the next part of my story without mentioning the Partition - the partition of what was once one country, India, into India and Pakistan in 1947. I was based in Roorkee, a cantonment about 100 miles North of Delhi, in what is called Uttar Pradesh (United Provinces or U.P.) The majority of our recruits came from the Punjab - Punjabi Musselmans or Sikhs - and it was in the Punjab that the worst of the carnage occurred. Hindus living in the Punjab who found themselves on the wrong side of the new boundary were largely killed - the same applied to the Mohammedans finding themselves in the new India. It was estimated that in the region of two million people lost their lives at the time of Partition and this was felt very keenly by the Bengal Sappers and Miners, to which I was attached, who recruited largely from the Punjab. In view of this,

India 1945/1948

it has always amazed me that the armies of India and Pakistan were able to bring things under control and also that we as a country are still on very friendly terms with both India and Pakistan. Long may it continue.

B 12 Platoon B Coy 1 T.B. R.I.E.

Chapter 2

DEMOB.   1948 -1955

We, demob group 59, arrived back in England in 1948 on board the Otranto. Now Captains, we were housed on a Mess deck in three tier bunks whereas on the way out in 1945 we were placed in first class cabins, two to a cabin, with no expense spared. However, we were coming home at last having been away for three years with no home leave so little things like that didn't worry us - just that when we went off to war we were treated right royally, but on the way back, who cared!

We arrived in Southampton and as we drew up alongside (or whatever the correct nautical term might be) there were crowds of relatives lining the quayside. We were all packed against the rails looking for our relatives - in my case, my parents - while they were to us a mass of faces as we inched our way to the dockside. I looked and looked to see if I could see them but to no avail. They, on the other hand, had seen me but could not draw my attention. So my father decided he had to do something so he shouted at the top of his voice - "Mark over" - I immediately spotted them! Not that I could meet them properly as we were packed into trains to our demob centre to get our civilian clothes - a suit, shoes, underwear, etc. My shoes lasted many years.

Demob 1948/1955

My father had invested in a racehorse after the war but like most racehorses, this one couldn't go fast enough so he bequeathed her to me as soon as I got home. It was a mare, name long forgotten and I was persuaded to resume hunting which we had all done as kids. After the war, when hunting re-started, there was very little in the way of hunt jumps or hedges, everything that could have been ploughed for food had been ploughed and so the field had to go from gate to gate or, in the case of the Tedworth, from Cannings gate to Cannings gate. The fields were small by today's standards and mostly female and while this may have seemed to possess intriguing possibilities it turned out rather differently. As the only young male out, guess who had to get off to open and shut all the wretched Cannings gates (made of wire and sticks for the uninitiated). As you can imagine, this soon palled - I gave up hunting, the horse was sold and I didn't resume until our children started riding.

Shooting was the first field sport I took up seriously on my return. I had a black Labrador before I joined the Army in 1943 and all the time I was away he was looked after by my father's keeper, known to all as Keeper Clarke. He used to have a pony to get around the farm - about 3500 acres - and my dog, whose name coincidentally was Jock as Keeper Clarke was a very broad Scot, accompanied him on his rounds. He was my first dog and was as wild as you could possibly imagine! My first game book which started in 1950 includes an entry for 25 November 1950 which reads "Also 2 rats, killed by Jock". Later, on 27 October 1951 I see "Jock, 1 hare" and on 3 November 1951 "Jock, 1 stoat". But he was my first dog and retains a special place in my memory.

Demob 1948/1955

Keeper Clark with Jock 1943

Jane and I were married on 14 April 1950, so this period of my life was very eventful. We had known each other since 1936 when I first went to a prep. school in Canford Cliffs called The Old Ride and although we didn't see each other from 1939, when I left The Old Ride (TOR) until after I came back from India I had craftily kept in touch by writing occasionally to Jane's father who was the headmaster of TOR. So we soon met up again and the rest is history, as they say!

To Jane, field sports have never been a great attraction. She had bought herself a horse before we were married but never hunted although they used to hold the Whaddon Chase Hunt Ball at TOR which by this time had moved to Little Horwood in Buckinghamshire. The hounds met there quite often and coincidentally one of the Masters used to come as a guest to Rushall when Herbert Blagrave rented the shooting. Another guest of Herbert Blagrave one day was Sir Gordon Richards, the well-known jockey. At the time we had a groom/handyman at The Manor, Upavon where we lived for the first 47 years of our married life, who had been apprenticed at Manton with Sir Gordon and in fact had started on the very same day. I had already heard from Burt Pateman, for that was his name, about his apprenticeship, so I asked Sir Gordon during the day if he would have time to have a word with Pateman before he went home. "Of course" he said so I took him over to Upavon after the shoot and I was talking to him as we went down the garden path towards Pateman who was digging with his back to us. "I would know that voice anywhere" he said before turning round to greet Sir Gordon. I have often wondered about those two men - both gentlemen - who started together but finished up so far apart. Luck? Fate? What?

So I tried to get Jane interested in shooting and my game book shows that while she was successful, I was not! On 2nd November 1950 we went duck shooting in the water meadows and she had one shot and got one duck. I thought I was winning so we went out again on the 4th November and she had another

Demob 1948/1955

shot and another duck. I thought I had won! But no, she never shot again although she would come out shooting with the guns on shooting days and acted as my loader/poker-in on our big day.

This reminds me of my attempt to interest her in salmon fishing. In May 1975 we took the car to Norway for a holiday and as I had been told trout fishing in Norway was all free, I took along a fly rod. We landed in Bergen and after a few nights in the Norge Hotel we motored up the Hardanger fiord to Voss and stayed in an hotel in the mountains. It was a big place but virtually empty as it was too early in the season for tourists so we spent our time exploring the locality. One day we went to the end of Voss lake and I started fishing the "osen" (outfall) for trout. By and by I hooked a fish and as I landed it (a sea-trout kelt) a Norwegian came out of his fishing hut, took it off the hook, killed it, said it was no good and took it away - to eat, presumably! I went with him into his hut and he showed me photographs of enormous salmon that he had caught in the Voss lake and/or river - his English was very rudimentary and my Norwegian was non-existent. But my interest was aroused and when we got back to our hotel I asked the manager if there was any salmon fishing available. He said he had none but that if he heard of any rods going he would get in touch with me in England.

Three weeks later I had a call to say that there were two rods available on the Voss at Bolstad for four days in June. I persuaded my wife to come with me and the result of that expedition was four fish averaging 30 lbs. of which Jane caught one of 23 lbs. Again I thought that she would be converted - but no, and although she occasionally will cast a spinner her

11

Demob 1948/1955

heart is not in it. But no-one can say I didn't try! This was the beginning of my Norwegian adventures - of which more later - and we have always found Norway a delightful country and the people very friendly and hospitable.

Throughout the early 1950's we always had a white hare on the North end of the farm at Upavon. Whether it was one getting older or young ones following on we never did discover, but I see from the game book that there is no reference to a white hare after 1955. It is surprising that it lasted as long as it did as it could be seen from a very long way away.

Arthur Belcher (A.B.) was a retired bank manager from Cirencester and he came to live with his wife in one of our houses in Rushall and acted as farm secretary to both farms for many years. He was very keen on shooting and always came out as a walking gun and organised the beaters' beer and such-like duties. And he was my "poaching" partner on Saturday afternoons for the early years before I had started hunting again when Saturdays were always kept for hunting. Anyway, on 26 November 1955 we were both invited by David Lemon to experience a day over Jim Maurice's red setters. Although by this time I had owned several labradors I had never been out with setters but as we had heard a lot about Jim's we felt we ought to dress for the part by putting on plus-fours. We duly arrived and set out and were instructed by Jim on how to behave. David was with us, making three guns, and Jim was working the setters. David still had a dairy then and the first field we went into was a grass ground on which they had scattered a load of cabbages for the cows to eat later. We were told to keep very quiet and wait until the setters froze when we were to form an arc round the setters when Jim would tell them to flush the pheasant. In due course the setters froze, pointing towards one of the cabbages which were pretty big so we quietly took our positions with loaded guns ready to deal with the quarry. Jim instructed the setters to flush the bird and we waited expectantly. Nothing appeared, so by and by Jim went up to the cabbage and as nothing moved he kicked the cabbage over - when a mouse shot out and disappeared! By this time you can imagine that the "guns" had been reduced to a fit of the giggles, much to the annoyance of Jim. However, I see from my game book we finished up with three pheasants and a teal and my remark in the last column was - "A day over setters - an education!"

This day was also involved with the "Cat Saga" which came about as follows, here recalled by Jane.

At a drink party one winter's evening David Lemon and I were discussing, for some extraordinary reason, the miracle of the loaves and fishes. David was convinced there were three fishes in the story, while I was certain that there were only two. I think we had some sort of bet. In any case we agreed to study our respective bibles on our return home, and David promised me a bottle of Chanel No. 5 if I was right.

A few days before Christmas a small parcel arrived in David's handwriting which I duly put away with other presents. Imagine my surprise and suspicion when another parcel was delivered the following day in the same handwriting. On opening it I discovered two herrings!

Somehow Barry and I felt this should not be the end of the story, so the fish were returned to the Lemon household surreptitiously. They were now becoming rather high.

Unfortunately perhaps, Barry had a shooting invitation with David a day or two later. On driving home he noticed an appalling smell and on

Demob 1948/1955

investigation found the remains of two herring on the exhaust pipe, burnt to a frazzle. I think David thought he had had the last word.

The fish were not mentioned on our next meeting with the Lemons, the intention being to convey the idea that we had never discovered the fried fish. However Wookeys do not give up easily and on New Years Eve the perfect opportunity arose.

After all these years I am slightly ashamed of the rest of the story, but at the time it seemed the logical way out. We had a close neighbour who kept nine cats. They frequently invaded our garden, and often "serenaded" us outside our bedroom window. On New Years Eve we were just about to get into the car to join friends in Marlborough at the Ailesbury Arms when one of these moggies crossed our path. On my encouragement Barry got out his gun and dispatched it. We then put the cat in a box, wrapped it in Christmas paper, attached a suitable label, saying that the cat had eaten the fish and died, and took it to Marlborough. To our delight David's car was parked in the centre of the High Street and unlocked!

During the New Years celebrations one of us happened to mention to the Lemons that we had left their Christmas present, which we had forgotten to give them, in the boot of their car. David seemed suitably surprised and grateful, and went off to open his present!

It was a very merry evening and after the Lemons and the Wookeys had had a good laugh over the whole affair some way had to be found to dispose of the "body". David hit on the idea of putting it in the bed of the hotel manager, who was very rude and unpopular, so he and Barry crept off to carry out the evil deed.

In all the excitement of the evening we had failed to notice that the box which the men put under the manager's bed, had Barry's father's address on the outside, so the next day there was some explaining to do!

Demob 1948/1955

This reminds me of a letter I had from Jimmy Hills after a day's fishing at Testwood - quite a coincidence!

"You must have thought me very greedy for accepting the large salmon, but in point of fact, with a multitude of 30 coming to lunch before the fete, the present of a loaf and a large fish was too opportune that it took on an almost biblical significance and completely solved the problem - and by jove they all enjoyed it."

Chapter 3

PARKER 1953-1959

Until 1953 we had been shooting at Upavon with Keeper Clark doing the keepering. He was, by this time, well past retiring age and his health was deteriorating with the result that very little keepering was being done. The annual bags of partridges show this decline:

1942/1943	165 Partridges
1943/1944	408
1944/1945	404
1945/1946	492
1946/1947	304
1947/1948	364 No rearing – all wild English partridges

These were the years when no sprays were being used.
1948 – 1953   69, 0, 50, 51 and 68

Keeper Clark died in 1953.

At about this time the Game Research Establishment came into being and they were doing a great job at Fordingbridge trying to re-establish partridges on farm land. My father knew Doug Middleton, the director, and when we came to thinking of a new keeper Doug Middleton suggested a young man from Damerham - Gordon Parker. With his appointment in 1953 we entered a decade of wild English partridge shooting at its very best. It was Gordon Parker's hard work, enthusiasm and know-how which made this possible, and the history of these ten years is a permanent monument to his success. Quite simply, without him we should never have achieved what we did.

This chapter, as far as shooting goes, deals with the first few years of his work with us. Vermin control was his first priority,. followed by nest finding and protection. At both he was superb and I learnt most of what I know about the English partridge from him. Partridge keepering is a most daunting task when you consider the perils a partridge has to contend with to bring up a covey of young. It is worth noting the enemies of the partridge as it makes you wonder how they have survived as long as they have. The vermin list includes Rats, Feral Cats, Stoats, Foxes, Weasels, Hedgehogs, Rooks, Jackdaws, Crows, Magpies, Little Owls, Grey Squirrels, Badgers, Buzzards, Kestrels, Sparrow Hawks and Jays. When you add farm vehicle damage to nests, human interference and haymaking, you can imagine the heartache a keeper suffers as he strives to produce a surplus to shoot. One of the most bizarre examples of partridge mum's problems was to see eight day-old partridge chicks in a cart rut - dead by starvation as they were unable to climb out.

Foxes are often a bone of contention in the world of field sports. Being a hunting man, my first instruction to Gordon Parker was always to have a fox for the hounds when they met on our land and I can safely say that during his stay that was always the case (though they may have taken a bit of finding on occasion!) Over the years, good keepers have controlled vermin - they do not exterminate it. Rats, possibly, are the exception as nobody likes rats and nobody would mind very much if they

17

disappeared completely. Nowadays, of course, there is no excuse for rats to be a nuisance as with the advent of warfarin it is very easy to keep them under control. But at what cost? The word hypocrisy springs to mind - many fanatical L.A.C.S. supporters devote their lives (and their money) to campaign against the hunting of foxes, who are either killed instantly or escape altogether, while they are silent on the deaths of millions of rats which die a long, lingering and painful death by poison. Badgers are another problem. Before the recent legislation, man kept them under control as they have no natural enemies in this country. Keepers would allow the odd badger sett to thrive but would draw the line at new setts being established in unacceptable places - i.e. near a rearing field. Now that you can go to prison for killing a badger they have multiplied very rapidly and the only (legal) way of controlling them is to run over them with your car. Does not a badger maimed by a car suffer infinitely more as it crawls away to die than a fox killed by hounds? How stupid can we get?

For Christmas 1952, my father gave me a lovely game book to coincide with the start of the Parker era. As he was a farmer, he always wrote in any book he gave us the initials G.S.P. - God Speed the Plough - and this game book was no exception. He also wrote "Hoping you will have many years of good sport to record" and at the bottom "It is always better to be SAFE than SORRY." Wise words indeed.

As there were several blank pages at the front of the book I thought it would be a good idea to ask all our guns to sign it when they came to shoot. We did this for many years and there are five pages filled with signatures, in several instances containing three generations of the same family, and many containing two. The total number of names is 194 and this does not include any let days as during these years all our local shoots were private, mostly farmer run.

After these pages of signatures, there are two pages devoted to our red-letter days (I entered them in red ink at the time as I thought each one would be the highest bag we were ever likely to achieve). I asked all the guns at the end of the day to sign a special column for that day and it is very interesting (at least it is to me!) to see who came on each day. My father invited half the guns and I invited the other half and Arthur Belcher always carried a gun, making a total of eleven guns. The red letter days falling in the period of this chapter (to 1959) occurred on 19 October 1956, 9 November 1956, 4 October 1957, 11 November 1958, 6 October 1959 and 6 November 1959. As only one red letter day occurred after this date I will include it here, 7 October 1960 to show how local and/or regular our guns were at that time.

The following were present on each of the above days: C.P. Wookey, David Lemon, Paul Hayward, Arthur Belcher, Harry Horton and C.B. Wookey. The bags were progressive as I only entered our then record days:

19 October 1956	195 br. Partridges
9 November 1956	308 Pheasants
4 October 1957	229 br. Partridges
11 November 1958	338 Pheasants
6 October 1959	334 ½ br. Partridges
6 November 1959	392 Pheasants + 10 br. Partridges
7 October 1960	520 ½ br. Partridges

Parker

The question as to who was our best local shot is often asked and, although everyone can shoot really well sometimes, only the best do so all (or most) of the time. As a local farmer and a good shot himself, Jack Wroth, once said to me, the best shot is the one who never misses an easy bird. However that may be, my choice of all our guests would have to be Paul Hayward, now sadly no longer with us. Not only was he a good shot, he had style and made it all look so easy. He was also a real gentleman as this story shows. He was shooting with a friend of ours - Stanley Haines at Milton, near Pewsey - where their best drive was from a beech belt on top of a steep hill - a hanging as we call it in Wiltshire. The centre guns had most of the pheasants over them and they were seriously high. On this particular day my friend, who was not a regular gun, was in the thick of it and wasn't getting on at all well and didn't touch one. Suddenly in the middle of the drive a good partridge came over and my friend killed it properly. After the drive, Paul, who had been an outside gun, watching it all, walked over to my friend and congratulated him on killing such a good partridge - with not a word about the missed pheasants. Not many would have done that.

It was about this time that I was persuaded to start riding again. Our children had just acquired a pony and Jim Read, the son of Monty Read, our local M.F.H. said that if the children were riding I would have to as well so he lent me a horse to get started. When I say horse, I suppose he was a horse but not one to be proud of! He was a grey, about 17 h.h. and strong enough to carry all the family! His feet were huge - as was everything about him, but he was a horse and I started riding. Whether I should have thanked Jim for the loan or refused I don't really know but taking the long view, I think I should thank him because we have had a long association with a lot of young horses, and we have thoroughly enjoyed them.

Another man instrumental in getting me interested in horses was Bill Hobbs. We met in Switzerland on one of our skiing trips and the first evening we went down to the bar to have a drink. We were perched at one end of the bar and we saw this couple, Bill and Lynette, sitting at the other end. We were both eyeing each other and we both, as we later discovered, thought that the others looked like farmers so we ought to get together. So we did and we became great friends until his untimely death. He was a great horseman - and a great gentleman - and found us several horses. He taught me many things about horses - one of the most useful when we later had a lot of young horses to back and school, was to make sure they had no shoes on when first being ridden and to get them onto the stoniest ground you could find! He hunted with the Warwickshire and we went up several times to have a day with them - but I couldn't follow him across country! He came down to shoot with us in November 1959 and his thank-you letter included an invitation to hunt with him and "to send your horses up together so that you and the girls can stay and make merry with us". We did and I remember we had roast beef and the best horseradish sauce that I have ever tasted - made by Lynette.

Throughout the 1950's and 1960's I always had a gun dog - usually black Labrador dogs - and I used to train them myself. Rather like breaking horses, dog training was a secret world to me until I came across a book called "Dog Training by Amateurs" by Richard Sharpe. First published in 1924, he was purported to be the first dog trainer to use a carrot instead of the stick. The first paragraph of the Foreword encapsulates this philosophy perfectly. "Perhaps the most striking feature of this book, and the one that will most appeal to the comparative novice, is the ease with which the more common and annoying faults in a shooting dog may be prevented from developing. How insuperable appears the difficulty of checking seeming perverseness, yet how easy the course of right development when once the journey has been mapped out." I have lent the book to numerous friends (and I still have it!) and they have all said how useful they found it. In my own case, when I started using his methods I had good success but later on when farming pressures built up, I tried to take short cuts with the result that my later dogs were not so reliable as the earlier ones.

"A child can do it!"

Parker

I did depart from the "black lab only" sequence when I tried out a couple of golden retrievers, father and son, Brutus and Bruno. They were lovely dogs of the heavier strain, unlike June Atkinson's which were much more wiry, but they did not have as long a useful life as the Labs.

Learning to retrieve fish

I recall two instances which stand out in my memory, both concerning Brutus. In his younger days he always came with us when we were exercising the horses and he developed a remarkable skill in locating and carrying hedgehogs. In those days there were many hedgehogs around and were classified as vermin as they liked nothing better than a partridge's nest full of eggs. So we would dismount and kill the hedgehog and then

23

proceed on our way. On this occasion when we looked round to see where he, Brutus, was we saw him trotting along carrying not one but TWO hedgehogs in his mouth. To carry one must be difficult enough - to carry two at once - unbelievable if we had not seen it.

The other instance was on a warm shooting day in early October. We were on dry downland and one of the guns had marked a partridge down to a certain spot but could not find it. Now every shooting man knows that there are some guns who are more optimistic than others and if you have a dog you may be asked to look for a fictitious bird, especially if the gun in question is having an off day! However, in this case the gun was "reliable" and everyone came to look for this bird on ground that was seemingly bare. All the dogs had a go, all the guns looked, but to no avail. I had Brutus with me, more as a spectator than active participant as by this time he was pretty old. So I came up and said I would give the old dog a try, so I went to the spot that had been indicated and said "Hi lost" more in hope than expectation. He started sniffing around, at a walk as he couldn't make extravagant casts as the younger dogs were doing and after a few moments I saw he had winded something. Very slowly he worked upwind and after about three yards up jumped the partridge and ran away. Brutus sat down (with a smirk on his face!) and let the other dogs do the chasing. The old Army adage, "if you don't want to be seen, don't move" was never more elequently demonstrated.

With the horses I was lucky in having two mentors when it came to breaking them in. Again, as with dogs, breaking horses was a closed book to me and I thought only a very few favoured people could cope. So first I turned to the BHS (British Horse

Society) pamphlet on the subject and was told to take the young horse into a small field and start lunging it. It sounded so simple so I tried it, only to find that the horse towed me round the field or that the horse was lunging me! So after a few hours of this I gave up and sought some practical help from, first of all, Brig. Jimmy Hills, ex Royal Horse Artillery, who had retired to the Old Vicarage at Easton Royal, near Pewsey. When I explained my problem he told me that I had to have a ring so that the horse couldn't escape me and I would have an outside boundary to keep the horse in. He also said I should use voice commands as in the Army and with his help I managed to break my first youngster, Hamlet, who would, after a few weeks, go through all his paces, up and down, in the ring on voice alone (no lunge rope). We have used this method ever since and have only had one horse, Frank, that defeated us. We bought him as a yearling at one of the Malvern Sales, a chestnut colt that didn't look too bad and was cheap (big mistake). We had no problem until we came to back him and then he didn't want to know. We tried a sack of corn tied to the saddle, but he just bucked and kicked until he got rid of it, ditto a rider. So we gave up and sold him at one of our sales as unbackable. He was bought, surprisingly, in spite of this and the buyer told me he could deal with him. A year or so later I met him somewhere and asked him how he was getting on. He said he had managed to stay on until Frank suddenly took off and galloped wildly round the field and the only way he could stop him was to point him at an unjumpable hedge - high and thick - in which Frank buried himself. I think he, the buyer, gave up after that!

We should, perhaps, have been warned that all was not well as when we went to collect him from his box on the Malvern

Showground we found the door broken down and the box empty. We had noticed a horse galloping round the showground but thought someone else was having trouble! Anyway, we eventually rounded him up, thanks to Frank Pearson from the New Forest and loaded him up. Hence his hame - Frank - as that year's intake were all named with a name starting with F. Incidentally, we started in 1975 with A's and currently have one Z - Zeus. Someone kindly suggested we should start again with some A's but his mathematics was not very good!

The other person who helped me with the young horses was the retired commandant of Imber Court, the Training establishment for the Metropolitan Police Horses. (His name was Harry Griffin, who had come to live in a neighbouring village) and his experience was also very useful to us in dealing with the young horses and I believe that it was his input that caused so many people over the years to comment on the good temperament of our horses. Another great help was one of the farm men who came to us from a racing stable, Badger Perrett, who once said "There is no such thing as a bad horse - they are only made bad". Another of Badger's remarks, which on the face of it seems rather nonsense but which I have come to believe to be very true over the years, was "A young horse learns as much when he is turned out after a few weeks training as he does from the actual training." I know it sounds daft but I know there is truth in it.

I mentioned earlier that my father knew Doug Middleton of the Game Research Establishment at Fordingbridge and it is, I think, interesting to note that as soon as December 1953, towards the end of Parker's first season, he, Middleton was writing to ask for bird samples. He wrote "We have recently been going into the literature concerning the effects of deficiencies in trace elements on the health of farm animals, and it seems that there is a line of enquiry worth following in relation to partridges ... I am trying therefore to get samples, for spectroscopic examination, from "healthy" and "unhealthy" areas. This involves the spectroscopic analysis of blood, and I wonder if it is possible for you to let us have, say, two brace of partridges, preferably young, for this purpose ... we are anxious to follow up any line which may throw light on the disastrous decline in the partridge population that has occurred on many areas during the past few years. Your ground, on which Parker is keepering, would seem to be a fine example of the right conditions for partridge survival, so a sample from there might prove very valuable." It should be remembered that Middleton was in charge of what was then the ICI Game Research Establishment and no reference is made to the real reason for the decline of the partridge - namely, starvation of the young chicks by destroying the weeds in corn fields on which the insects, essential to a young partridge's survival in the first three weeks of life, feed. This indirect effect was one of the three things that persuaded me to change over to an organic system of farming, as set out in my book **"Rushall, the story of an organic farm."** The relevant chapter is reproduced at Appendix A.

Another set of statistics - Nest and Hatch Records: Upavon and Littlecott: 1954 - is reproduced at Appendix B. It just shows the amount of work put in by Parker to achieve what he did on the Upavon and Littlecott beats. I include it as it shows how different gamekeeping is today from what it was even as late as the 1950's and 1960's. It reminds me of the story of some foreign potentate's shoot which was late starting. So the big wig summoned his keeper and demanded to know why they couldn't start shooting. The keeper replied " I am very sorry, my Lord, but the train is late."

Chapter 4

RECORD PARTRIDGE DAY

The 7th October 1960 was the day we shot 520 ½ brace of partridges and I feel that it was such a wonderful occasion that it merits a chapter to itself. I am grateful to T.H. Blank of the Game Research Station for his account of the day written for Shooting Times and County Magazine in September 1978. He also wrote a letter on 11 October 1960 when obviously his memory was much clearer so I include both, as well as a few of the letters received afterwards.

But of course it wasn't just the 7th October 1960. The build up to this memorable day started with Gordon Parker's appointment in 1953. I have already set out the red-letter days but there were, of course, many other memorable days and I quote from my Game Book.

Total partridges for season:

16 October	1953	Our first 100 br. day		726
8 October	1954	83 br. partridges		369
7 October	1955	129 br. partridges		767 + 274 pheasants
19 October	1956	188 br. partridges		1042 + 523 pheasants
4 October	1957	229 br. partridges	*	1294 + 921 pheasants
10 October	1958	183 br. partridges		910 + 905 pheasants

Record Partridge Day

6 October	1959	334 ½ br. partridges		1674 +1072 pheasants
4 December	1959	113 ½ br. partridges		* see note below
7 October	1960	520 ½ br. partridges		2232 +1285 pheasants
2 October	1962	141 br. partridges	)	
12 October	1962	128 br. partridges	)*	884 + 1214 pheasants
16 October	1962	110 br. partridges	)	

*While we were enjoying wonderful shooting during the Parker era, there were two things I wanted to achieve. The first was the "Autumn Treble" where we would shoot 100 br. on three separate days as the whole farm lent itself to division into three separate beats although, of course, with only one keeper. In spite of having good stocks of partridges, achieving three separate days of 100 br. on our downland was not easy - so many things can defeat you. The weather, how the guns are feeling, a peregrine, buzzard or harrier on the beat and how the birds decide to behave. So we were very pleased to be able to do it twice - in 1957 and 1962.

The other aim was to shoot 100 br. in December. By December the birds are strong and very wild, much of the cover has disappeared and they are easily spooked. The drives have to be much larger as the birds fly so much further once they are disturbed - very similar to grouse drives in September/October. Anyway, we eventually achieved this on the 4th December 1959 and the entry in my Game Book reads: "In its way, as great an achievement as the 6th October. Vast drives, masses of birds and first class shooting. As someone said - a moderate team of guns would have had a job to kill 30 br. - Eight partridge drives, one of them a field of 24 acres".

One of those days when everything goes right!

Record Partridge Day

To produce a huge number of wild birds is the key to large bags but of almost equal importance is the layout of the farm. On our downs, with many small valleys, it is ideal shooting country provided there is sufficient holding cover to collect the birds. Roots were the favoured cover at Upavon, preferably turnips as their rough leaves don't hold the rainwater as do swedes, rape or kale. Of course, if you have a good admixture of weeds this makes the cover even better! The cover crops had to be situated on high ground in front of the line of butts which led to some of our fields seemingly in perpetual root crops, not good farming practice but very good for partridge shooting!

Before every partridge day we would have a briefing session with the key beaters and transport drivers. Parker and I would have decided the order of drives beforehand so at the briefing we would have the two flankers and go through each drive in detail so all the key people would know just where to go. Parker would control the beaters and I would see to the guns and if all went well everything would go according to plan! Sometimes the guns would be late taking up their stands and birds would be coming over before they were ready - but that didn't happen to any gun more than once! My secretary would type out five copies of the day's order of drives - one for Parker, one for me, one for each flanker and one for the tractor driver - with all the details about transport and starting points. This may sound a bit complicated but it worked pretty well.

After the briefing for the big day, I went round to Parker's house to go over the final details. We knew we had a lot of birds and we had let it be known that the guns might like to bring a "poker-in" to help them as we always used single guns. We both felt that this was to be our best day yet and we both put down what we thought the bag would be, without showing our figure to the other. I jotted down my figure - 500 br. - in my diary and after it was all over I asked Parker what he had put down - and it was the same!

Before asking you to read the account of the day by T.H. Blank, there are three incidents to record. The first occurred at The Manor as the guns were assembling. One of them, John French, who was my best man on 14 April 1950 and was also at school with me, opened his gun case and took out his gun to assemble it. As I happened by I saw him blowing down the barrels to clear a mass of cobwebs that had accumulated since last he had used it! He lived in Kent and was keener on cricket than shooting but in spite of his evident lack of practice he could still shoot.

The second incident was our arrival at the first drive. Peter Horton, our neighbouring farmer and local M.F.H. (Tedworth Hunt) climbed out of his Land Rover only to discover that he had left his gun at home! He dashed home to get it and dashed back only to find that the drive was over and we had shot 75 br. You should have seen his face! His place had been taken by our walking gun, Arthur Belcher, who had had a wonderful drive - you should have seen his smile!

And the third incident was at lunch time when we were counting the bag. I had arranged for a tractor and trailer to meet us at the Field Barn, where we were lunching, to take the morning's bag back to The Manor as I figured that the usual game-cart would be unable to take 500 br. The tractor drivers were swapping the birds into the relief cart and counting them. When I asked how many we had had in the morning they gave me a figure which, after a bit of mental arithmetic, I felt had to

Record Partridge Day

be wrong. So we counted them again - I do not recall the actual figures - and discovered that they had miscounted by 100 br! When I think of the times we have struggled to get 100 br. in a whole day, to miscount by 100 br. on this day somehow put the whole thing into perspective.

Before reading T.H. Blank's account of the day, the following is his letter written to my father a few days after it happened.

I.C.I. Game Services
GAME RESEARCH STATION . BURGATE MANOR FORDINGBRIDGE . HAMPSHIRE
Telephone: FORDINGBRIDGE 2381

11th October, 1960.

C.P.Wookey Esq.,
Rushall Manor,
Pewsey,
Wilts.

Dear Mr. Wookey,

Thank you very much indeed for a most enjoyable and most memorable day.

Never have I seen such numbers of partridges, and I am sure that had you wished to turn a delightful sporting day into a marathon, you could have doubled the bag. To the onlooker the surprising thing was that the bag was so large - the numbers shot seemed to make no impression on the masses of birds going over! This is no reflection on the high quality of the shooting,

Record Partridge Day

but does emphasise the relatively small proportion of the total partridge population that has so far been shot.

My only regret was the poor quality of the light - I should have liked to have had a photographic record of some of those large packs going over. I did manage to get just over 50 on the enclosed snap but the lengthy exposure resulted in a blurred picture.

Thank you once again, and congratulations for showing that, with good farming and good keepering, partridges can be as numerous as they have ever been.

Yours sincerely,

T. H. Blank.

In a year such as this when there will be precious little partridge shooting for anyone in the southern half of England it might be a suitable time to recall a memorable partridge day that occurred in Wiltshire, 18 years ago. In fact, it was a record day for this part of England, since more than 500 hundred brace of partridges were shot. Not that there is anything very creditable in numbers themselves so much as the fact that wild partridges were sufficiently numerous to allow such a bag to be made against the background of modern agriculture. Let it not be thought that an unduly heavy toll was taken on the day - for no real attempt at records was being considered. Indeed, there were enough partridges left to shoot a further thousand birds on subsequent days and still leave sufficient to provide an excellent breeding stock for the following spring. If the surplus partridges are there they should be shot - and from a management viewpoint the sooner the crop is harvested the more food and living room is left for the overwintering survivors. That the maximum number of partridges should be present for the minimum amount of time - i.e. until they are old enough to be "cropped" - is a sound but often impractical maxim.

By the middle 50s the grey partridge was generally on the decline - and yet in 1960, on October 7, 520 brace of partridges (all but 15 of them grey partridges) were shot. How did this come about? The shoot at Upavon of approximately 3,500 acres mostly owner-farmed by the late Mr C. P. Wookey had been keepered for many years. But in 1952 Gordon Parker, then a young keeper who had learnt much from his earlier years as a beatkeeper under Bert Ambrose at the ICI's experimental shoot at Damerham (Fordingbridge), took charge as the single-handed keeper, and partridge bags steadily increased.

There is no secret about his methods. Like all really good partridge keepers he was an accomplished nest-finder. By effective control of nest predators, combined with skilful nest management he ensured that the maximum possible number of partridge nests hatched successfully. In his first season - which was fortunately blessed with suitable weather - a 100-brace day was achieved for the first time. And only once in the 12 ensuing seasons did they drop below this self-imposed standard while breeding stock were steadily increased. Then came the good weather years of 1959 and 1960. In the former, one of the best post-war partridge chick survival years, 1,674 partridges were shot with the best day yielding 334 brace. And still enough partridges were left to provide a very high breeding density

Record Partridge Day

(probably averaging a pair to every three or four acres) the following year.

And so the stage was set for 1960. A warm spring and summer up until late July had helped to produce an abundance of insects. Although the end of July and much of August was wet, the young partridges were old enough and sufficiently well fed and feathered to resist anything the weather might throw at them. Both nesting success and chick survival rates were exceptionally high and this resulted in one of the heaviest concentrations of partridges over a 3,000 acre area in post-war years - or indeed at any time in the past.

October 7, 1960 dawned grey and overcast with very little wind. The 10 guns together with an equal number of "pickers-up" gathered in the farmyard at 9 am. Meanwhile the 20 beaters were already taking up their stations for the commencement of the first of the morning drives. On this wide open rolling Wiltshire Countryside partridges cannot be driven on a narrow front and a line of 10 guns is necessary.

Although none of the guns had any thought of records in mind they all knew the ground carried an unusual number of partridges (cartridge-wise they had come suitably prepared). The team was a good one and Stanley Haines one of the most experienced of guns, had been warned that in the "catchment area" of the first drive there were approximately 100 coveys - and the keeper hoped to put at least 80 of them over guns in the first stand! In fact the first drive yielded 75 brace - and Stanley Haines had 37 birds down, picking all but two of them himself, before moving on to the next drive. For although the day was well organised there was no disturbing sense of urgency to mar the enjoyment of the day. There was time for the guns to work their dogs before the "pickers-up" took over.

At times there was a continuous stream of partridges crossing the line of guns as coveys snowballed into loosely knit packs.

Approximately 1,800 acres were driven over in the five morning and five afternoon drives. Each drive had its full quota of birds and the average bag of 50 brace per drive kept the attendants of the two game carts fully occupied. The last drive ended at 4.30 pm when, in early October, there is still plenty of light and time for the temporarily scattered coveys to reform and the birds to fill their crops before nightfall. By 5 o'clock, back at the game larder, the final tally had been made and the young/old ratio in the bag of approximately 4/1 confirmed the estimates of high chick survival rates. Just then the light rain, which the grey skies had threatened all day, began to fall gently and one of the most memorable partridge days in post-war years was over.

I was there - not as a gun of course, or the bag would never have reached the 500 brace mark! They were all good guns and I've recently refreshed my memory by discussing the day with two of them - Stanley Haines and Peter Hayward. Their ability to shoot those fast-flying Wiltshire downland partridges is equalled only by their love of the birds and knowledge of partridge behaviour and management. With memories of the last two (1977 and 1978) relatively disastrous partridge seasons in mind we asked ourselves how it could have happened that only 18 years ago partridges at Upavon were so numerous?

"Modern" farming was then well under way and herbicides and insecticides were widely used. Rabbits, who often buffered the effect of predators on partridges (and also kept the downland grasses short so that the yellow hill ant flourished) had long since practically disappeared. And yet, after the good partridge production year of 1959 breeding stocks were averaging a pair to little over three acres and even at this exceptionally high-density could produce an average of 10 surviving young per pair in August! It's true there was little or no aerial spraying of cereals against aphids in those days and unfortunately there are no records of general insect abundance at that time. Wide verges of the downland tracks and areas of rough grazing were probably rich sources of insect food for the partridge chicks. But, undoubtedly the key factor was the keeper.

Of course the habitat has to be suitable and the sequence of weather during spring and early summer conducive to the development of an abundant supply of suitable insect chick food. If these two pre-requisites are satisfied then the keeper's activities, by ensuring that the highly vulnerable sitting partridges hatch successfully, make all the difference. Gordon Parker's tireless predator control, his nest-finding ability and skilful manipulation of clutches ("dummying" dangerous nests and expediting hatches of nests in exposed situations, etc) produced the high nesting success that allowed the achievement of a chick survival rate as high as 5/1! Inevitably some nests were lost and the chicks from the bantam-incubated eggs had to be reared. But rearing, except as a salvage operation, played no significant part in the story and less than 200 partridges were released on the 3,000-acre area.

Pheasants were reared, however - about 1,000 of them every year. And how did this fit into the time absorbing programme of managing the wild partridges? Wasn't there here a distinct clash of interests? Of course there could have been. But by delaying his pheasant hatching until after June 25 (and ensuring that all his manipulated partridge nests were "chipped off" before that date) the keeper was able to give undivided attention to the management of his wild partridges and reared pheasants consecutively. It just meant that his period of working at full stretch was extended over a longer period than most people would have tolerated!

Incidentally, it was at Upavon that Gordon Parker developed his love of the redlegged partridge and reared his first broods in an area which is almost exclusively grey partridge country. Readers will know him better as the highly successful owner of the Astley Game Farm, which specialises in the production of pure redlegged partridges!

For the record, it was the Paul Hayward I have previously mentioned, not Peter Hayward as it appears in the article. And as Paul always wrote very nice "Thank you" letters, and this day was no exception, I reproduce his letter here:

Vicarage House,
Tidcombe,
Marlborough.

Oct.8 1960.

Dear Barry,
As the years go by and your bags increase you make it more and more difficult for me to find adequate adjectives to describe my gratitude and admiration.

Record Partridge Day

It is always a great pleasure to shoot at Upavon but yesterday it was also a great honour to be asked to shoot on a day in the like of which I thought only Kings and Dukes participated.

When my grandson sits on my knee in years to come I shall now be able to say how in the good old days I was out shooting when over 1000 partridges were killed in one day!

Anyway full marks to you and Gordon Parker for making such a memorable day possible, and may your game book records continue to mount!

Congratulations once again and all my thanks.

Yours ever,

Paul.

Incidentally, both my father and I always enjoyed shooting with Paul at Tidcombe. The days were always very well run with a good mixture of partridges and pheasants and some very good stands to show them. Paul had married into the Horton clan and he and David Lemon were brothers-in-law. One day David started choking on a sweet and for a minute or so it was a bit serious. But when he had recovered someone remarked that it was a good job it was a Polo with a hole in the middle and not a solid sweet!

One other letter I reproduce as it is from a keen shooting man with whom some of us used to go grouse shooting in Yorkshire - Scargill, near Greta Bridge. He was also the well known trainer from West Ilsley and a very good shot.

Record Partridge Day

"Thank you so very much for a wonderful days shooting - I've never seen so many partridges in one day in my life - never at any shoot have I enjoyed myself so much - partridges were flying over me most of the night! I shall look forward to Nov. 8th - again many, many thanks."

Chapter 5

SALMON AND TROUT

Joe Maggs, the previous owner of Rushall, was always very kind to me. Not only did he give me my first proper gun, a 20-bore, he also gave me my first fly rod as well as a fishing record book dated 1948. His enthusiasm was such that I had to keep on practising until I caught my first trout on a dry fly - 21st April 1948. I was a little worried about it as it only weighed 7 ozs. and I thought I should have put it back. However, a close friend of both families was at home when I came in with it and she said that Joe often caught them as small as that! I don't expect he did but it put my mind at rest.

Joe Maggs was pretty poorly in 1945 so he summoned my father and told him that he was going to sell Rushall and that he, my father, had got to buy it. There had been a disastrous fire in the main yard in the middle of Rushall, where we now live, and I think the worry of that plus his health made him decide to get out. Eventually my father bought it, Joe Maggs moved into The Lodge in the village, recovered and lived quite happily for another ten years. He came shooting with us on several occasions and I remember asking him one day what he would consider a good day's partridge shooting for any one gun. He shot a lot around the district and his considered answer was that he would have thought he had a good day if he shot 8 br. of partridges. Interesting!

While Joe Maggs, who, incidentally, was Chairman of United Dairies in those days, the saviour, I am told, of many small dairy farmers, it was another great character who started me on salmon fishing. My father never fished himself and when A.G. Street offered him a day at Testwood it was passed on to me. Arthur Street, farmer, author and broadcaster was a great raconteur and one day when we had Lord Rank to shoot on the same day there was a great tussle as to who could cap the other's stories! No prizes for guessing who won! The day they came together was the 14th October 1960, the week after our big day, and we shot 163 br. - enough to keep them both happy!

I was once invited to shoot at Sutton Scotney - pheasants - on 30 December 1960 and I recall the day for the washing facilities! When we went in to tea we were shown into the "gents" where there were 10 stalls, 10 handbasins and 10 towel rails! The house is now a Nursing Home and in its grounds has been built a Children's Hospice - Naomi House - for which I was involved with the fundraising. They employed a very personable girl called Emma who rang to arrange an appointment. Before I knew where I was I had been appointed Chairman of the Marlborough Fundraising Committee. There were committees like ours all round the South of England and I am pleased to say the Hospice is up and running. While I was dithering about whether to do it or not, I was propelled over the edge by my secretary saying "You have four healthy grandchildren".

But I digress - A.G. Street, another Arthur (Rank, Belcher, Street) had a day a month at Testwood, the lowest pool on the River Test and tidal. A.G.S. told me that if I could go down on

Salmon and Trout

the May day I would surely catch a fish. Not knowing any better I duly set off, picked him up from his home at South Newton (he also provided lunch) and so arrived at Testwood. In those days there were salmon aplenty and I duly caught one - 10 lbs. and very exciting it was. The ghillie, Terry, showed me how to mount and fish a prawn. All you had to do then was to stand by the "Boards" which were opposite the "Lion's Mouth" where the river flowed into the pool through hatches, and wait until you felt a knock when he told me to strike as quickly as I could. "Never hesitate before striking" he told me because "many more are lost by striking too slowly than too fast". That advice stood me in good stead in the years to come when I took a monthly rod on the death of A.G.S.

Testwood Pool

Salmon and Trout

It was ten years before I caught my second fish - also at Testwood! I went every year in May, either as the guest of A.G.S. or when I had a rod myself but ten years is a long time to come home after every fishing day and report yet another blank day. However, things started looking up when our boys became interested and looking through some of my records I see I have fished in many places (and in the sea at Mudeford). They include Testwood, the Wye, Blagdon, Chew (the lake boiled at 9.30 and we couldn't catch a thing) the Exe, the Lyon, the Tay and the Tweed, Two Lakes (my only fish was eaten by a rat!) the Blackwater on the Isle of Arran, Broadlands, the Hampshire Avon, the Easkey in Ireland, the Shin and probably some more which I can't recall at the moment. There are stories from each place that come to mind but I won't bore you with them all! Our best season at Testwood was 40 salmon in 1969. One occasion on the Wye as a guest of Bob Browning who I firmly believe to have fished every fishable river in the British Isles! I went to fish his beat at Hay on Wye one day and we had to cross a small field to reach the river bank. As I was crossing this field I espied a mound on my route and as I approached it was evident that it was a salmon. At the same time, a head appeared above the bank which turned out to be that of the other guest of Bob fishing there that day. As the fish was about 100 yards from the river I asked him how it had got there. Evidently, this was the first fish he had ever caught and he didn't want it to jump back into the river - I know how he felt!

As far as salmon fishing goes I am not a purist. Bob Browning, on the other hand, is. He is quite happy to flog away all day with his fly rod and he gets results - he is a very good fisherman. But the hunter instinct in me is still too strong - when I go salmon fishing I like to feel I am in with a chance and so am quite prepared to use any legitimate method - fly, spinning, bait - or worm! Obviously you can only use what is allowed on the water you are fishing but I must confess I like a bit of worming! With a fly, spinner or bait you get a bang and the fish is either on or off. With a worm you get a much longer period of suspense before you know whether you have hooked him or not. When anyone asks me how to worm for salmon (not many do as wormers are looked down on by the purists, most of whom, however, use a worm when necessary!), I tell them that they must be patient. When you feel the first little pluck or nibble, do NOT strike. Wait until you have counted 153 slowly and then strike. It works! In this way you get at least two and a half minutes of mounting excitement before you know he's on - the rest is pure mechanics. No doubt this is what prompted Joe Maggs to tell me one day that hooking a fish is everything - when he is on you should hand your rod to the ghillie to land it for you. Personally I do not subscribe to this theory because there is no greater thrill, to my mind, of landing a good salmon single-handed. But in Joe Magg's day there were probably so many salmon about that you would be worn out if you tried to land them all yourself!

When fishing at Broadlands one day I was talking to the head ghillie whose name was Bernard - I forget his surname - and he said something to me that I have never forgotten. He said "The day I don't get a thrill out of catching a salmon, I will give up fishing." I agree - mostly. The reason I hesitate is because nowadays many fisheries operate a "catch and release" system, where you have to return all (or most) of the fish caught. I know

Salmon and Trout

the reasoning is that you are conserving the stock while still having the fun of fishing, but to me that does not appeal. When I go fishing I like to take home at least some of my fish and I would rather not go if "catch and release" is the rule. I am also not convinced that the released fish do survive their ordeal - I have never seen any figures to prove that they do. There is a counter argument that say it is ethically wrong to "play" a fish out and then release it. Play is the operative word as we were always taught as boys that one must respect one's quarry. The choice is yours!

Catch of the day at Testwood

In April 1969 we went to Aberfeldy with the two boys for a fishing holiday. We stayed in the Dun Aluinn Hotel which was then owned by Maj. Stewart, a keen fisherman and he found us fishing on the Tay and the Lyon. The total catch was a single salmon caught by Steve, but the highlight of the trip was to have tea in the garden of Miss Ballantyne, the holder of the British rod caught salmon record - 64 lbs - and the boys were introduced to her. I wonder if there will ever be a bigger one?

The problem with fishing in the British Isles nowadays is that there are too many fishermen for the amount of water. This leads to the "put and take" fisheries which are necessary if the fishermen are to have a chance of catching something but it does detract from the pleasure of fishing when you know that your quarry was likely to have been swimming around a fish farm a few days ago. This is no criticism of the modern fisherman, the fishing owner or the fish farm - it is just sad that through no fault of their own they can seldom enjoy the purely wild fishing for our native brown trout that my generation was lucky enough to have had.

This may be the moment to state my personal adopted theory that every field sportsman has an inbuilt quota for each type of quarry he pursues. As a young man you tend to be a bit gung-ho and shoot (or fish) for the sake of it - and have great fun doing it. But as you get older you approach your "quota" and as this happens you become less enthusiastic to kill - whether it be shooting partridges and pheasants, catching salmon and trout or shooting a stag. Some people's "quota" may be different from others and they go on enjoying their field sports for as long as possible. For myself, and I appreciate that my generation in Wiltshire enjoyed the cream of partridge shooting, the urge to shoot left me some years ago and my guns were sold. I still have my fishing rods although I fish very little now, except for salmon when I get the chance. With hunting I suspect it is old age that is the determining factor rather than any "quota" but the result is the same. None of this should in any way be construed as a criticism of field sports, just that as one gets older there are other priorities - keeping alive, for one! I have really enjoyed my time with field sports and given the opportunity I would change nothing that I have done.

Chapter 6

TRIATHLON

This chapter is dedicated to the Reynolds family - Tom and Ursula - from N. Yorkshire. It was they, I am reliably informed, who dreamed up the idea of a sporting triathlon over dinner one night at their home in Melsonby. Their idea was to have a competition to draw together the three main branches of the British Field Sports Society (B.F.S.S.) with a view to creating a greater co-operation between the three sports. This was in the early 1970's when the campaign against hunting was beginning to gather momentum and they felt that if hunting was ever lost, the other two sports might well follow. Sadly, at that time, as hunting was the only sport being targeted, the other two were somewhat lukewarm in their support so this Triathlon was seen as a means of drawing the sports together. Like many good ideas, this one was not well supported by the B.F.S.S. and after Tom's retirement it sadly lapsed.

The competition was between teams of three who had to be composed of one member under 21, one lady and one over the age of 38. The young one and the "old" one could both be ladies but the team had to be of mixed sex - you could not have three men or three ladies. The competition itself consisted of three phases - fishing, shooting and riding and each had a set of rules devised by Tom and Ursula.

Triathlon

Tedworth Hunt Team
R to L David Horton, Joanna Horton and CBW

FISHING. This was divided into two parts - dry fly and wet fly. The targets in each case were five rings about 2 ft. diameter anchored at various distances from the casting platform. The fly was a short length of red wool tied to the end of the cast and the rod had to be no longer than 9 ft. The dry fly test was on accuracy. Three casts at each ring to score 3 points for a first hit, 2 for a second hit and 1 for a third hit, so you could score 6 points/ring or 30 in total. The wet fly was a speed contest - you had a minute to hit each ring in turn for 2 points each -

maximum 30 points. Thus the fishing maximum total was 60/member or 180/team.

SHOOTING. This was also out of a maximum of 60/member. Originally they used what is termed "springing teal". For those who have never shot at this variety of clay pigeon, as I hadn't, it consists of the clay being thrown upwards at an angle of 60 degrees or so from a point about 20 yards in front of the gun. When I first started in this competition I thought I could shoot a bit, but these birds completely defeated me so I had to go to a shooting school to learn the art! I think they used these springing teal for safety reasons as the novice shots, of which there were several, would with a bit of luck be firing towards the heavens. Later on, as the competition developed, crossing birds were used with each team shooting together and the number of birds missed were counted. And later still they introduced a few "bumble bees" (a very small clay) in each team's ration. I could never even see these, let alone shoot one so our best shot had to be on the left of the line to clean up the bumble bees as well as any of the others missed. This format was quite exciting as well as being quicker as each team shot together. Maximum total/team - 180.

RIDING. This was over a Handy Hunter type course and usually included a gate and/or an obstacle over which you had to lead your horse and then remount - not so easy for some! Again, this was originally an individual exercise with a maximum of 60/member but latterly (because watching a lot of not very good riders jumping in a ring was rather boring) it was a team effort. This meant the best horse going first as any knock down

Triathlon

removed that fence for the rest of the team. Maximum/team - 180.

Thus the total for any team was a maximum of 540 points.

Dressed for the Fishing phase

When I first joined the New Forest Team in 1974 the competition was being sponsored by Bernard Thorpe and

53

Partners who appointed a member of staff as their representative at the various shows we attended. They were tremendous sponsors and we spent many happy hours in their caravan emptying their bar of whatever drink they happened to have! I hope that their sponsorship was as beneficial to them as it was to the competition and the competitors who greatly enjoyed their hospitality. Other sponsors followed and we were indebted to them all but Bernard Thorpe and Partners were the first and helped to launch the whole show.

The competition was organised at shows throughout the country - I recall the Bath and West, Windsor, Welbeck Abbey - with the final being held at the East of England Show at Peterborough. Tom Reynolds was always present at the qualifiers replete with his bowler hat and stentorian voice, and was the backbone of the whole competition. The names of the teams are indicative of the spirit engendered by Tom and included the following:

> Lincolnshire Poachers
> Usk Grubs
> Sealed Knot
> The Good, the Bad and the Ugly
> Colchester R.C.
> Eire.

The other person who contributed largely to the success of the competition was the Chairman of the Committee - Tony Leavey. He was an ex-M.P. at the time I knew him and lived in London but he, too, was present at most of the qualifiers and certainly at the Zone and National Finals at Peterborough. The

Committee was one of the B.F.S.S. Sub-Committees and Tony helped steer it through to "acknowledged status" in the B.F.S.S., but not to "funded status". I remember he asked me to go to London one day for a meeting of the full B.F.S.S. Board/Committee to see if I could persuade them not only to recognise the Triathlon but also to fund it as a means of drawing all field sports together. I duly journeyed to London and waited. to be called by the great and the good of the B.F.S.S. When eventually I was ushered into the presence I could tell in a moment that they were only going through the motions of listening to my plea. I readily admit that I am no salesman but the people in that room were all, seemingly, M.F.H. of this or that pack and considered shooting and fishing vastly inferior to hunting. Indeed, the general criticism of the B.F.S.S. at that time was that it was run by hunting people for hunting and the name was slightly misleading. Anyway, after a few minutes they thanked me for coming and off I went - empty handed! It seemed to me then, and it still seems to me now, that they missed a great opportunity of drawing all field sports together to resist the attack on hunting, with others no doubt to follow.

The following is an extract from the B.F.S.S. Year Book for 1976.

THE BERNARD THORPE TRIATHLON.

In its 4th year the Triathlon maintained its steady growth with 63 teams competing. Among the 189 persons who practised for and competed in it there was a large proportion who were "having a go" at one of the three sports which they had not seriously tackled before. Besides bringing together shooting,

Triathlon

fishing and hunting people, the event undoubtedly generates an excellent spirit of keen but friendly competition, enhanced by its openness to all degrees of skill and experience. People like to take part for the fun of it.

The Grand Final was at the East of England Show at Peterborough on 22nd July. The winners were the New Forest Hunt Team with a score of 415 points out of 540. This team have been great supporters of the Triathlon since it was introduced in 1973 and they had finished second and third in previous years.

The winner of the special award for the best individual combined score was Mr. Barry Wookey with a score of 165 out of 180 for the member of the team over 38 years of age, and Mrs. Karen Pearson won the award for the best lady with a score of 139 out of 180.

The Republic of Ireland team won the Eley Perpetual Trophy and also Medals for the highest shooting score of 174 out of 180. Mr. Michael Strawson of the Lincolnshire Poachers team was the winner of the Eley High Gun medal.

For 1977 there will be twelve qualifying rounds, the two semi-finals and final will be held at the East of England Show, Peterborough on 19th, 20th and 21st July. In addition to prizes of two days' shooting, fishing and hunting, the winners will be awarded mementoes by Bernard Thorpe and Partners.

We were lucky enough on one occasion to win a day's grouse shooting with Lord Hartington as he then was (now The Duke of Devonshire) in Derbyshire. He was most generous and while some of us had shot grouse before, others had not and he went to great lengths to explain everything and we had a wonderful day. May the Triathlon return!

We ran a private Triathlon here at Rushall on 18 September 1976 and because of the difficulty for people finding a horse fit enough to jump at that time of year we devised two classes - Class I was the usual Riding, Fishing and Shooting and Class II was Archery, Fishing and Shooting.

We had quite a good turn out and I think everyone enjoyed themselves as is evidenced by this letter from one of our helpers:

September 19th, 1976.

Dear Barry and Jane,

I can't let yesterday's Triathlon go by without a word of praise and thanks to you both. The pleasure you give to so many people over the years with your different activities is quite superb and I am sure fully appreciated by all who partake in some form or other. There is something about Rushall that it difficult to describe but whenever I come there in whatever capacity it is a day you know you are going to enjoy. Not only is the setting superb, the organisation is beyond repute, and the weather is generally kind. Thank you both for all you do for so many of all ages and long may you continue to do so.

Yours ever,

Michael.

The Triathlon that we competed in reminds me of another ambition I had at that time - I had read about a

"McNab" which I understood to be the completion of another treble, in this case a stag, a grouse and a salmon, to be taken by one person on his own ground in one day. Realising that a McNab was impossible on our farms in Wiltshire I set myself the challenge of what I call "The Poor Man's Treble". This was to be a fox, a partridge (wild English) and a brown trout all to be taken on our land on the same day. The snag was, of course, that the fox had to be fairly hunted and killed by hounds but as I was never an M.F.H. that was impossible. When I was bragging about having achieved this one day in Peter Horton's hearing he turned and said "And who killed the fox?" So I had to compromise to the extent that the fox had to be found and accounted for on our land and I had to be riding to hounds at the time.

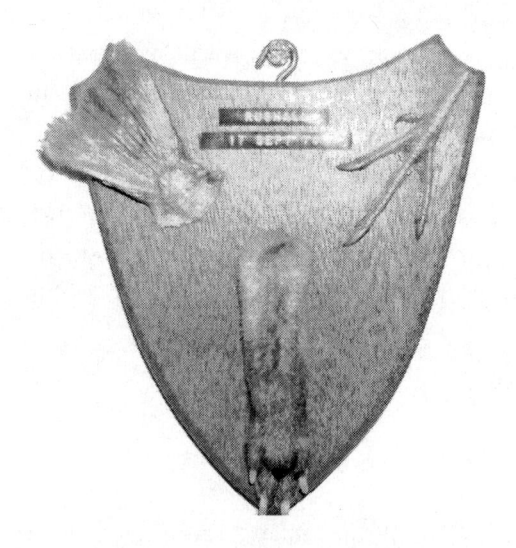

The "Poor Man's Treble"

Triathlon

I set out to do this on several occasions and the difficulty was the fox. The days were limited to the time all three were takeable on the same day so this meant between 1 September (the opening of the partridge season) and the 15th October (the close of trout fishing). The hounds were doing the annual cubbing - now called autumn hunting - which meant very early starts but as indicated above we did manage to achieve it on three occasions - 10 October 1968, 17 September 1974 and 9 September 1978. On each occasion, having killed the fox, the partridge was easy as we had a lot about at that time but the trout often proved difficult. On the second occasion, 17 September 1974, I see from my book that it "took all day to catch the trout." Perhaps this is why I took especial care to mount the trophies.

Chapter 7

NORWAY

The word Norway conjures up pictures in my mind of majestic mountains, huge rivers, mightly salmon and very friendly people. I visited it on sixteen occasions between 1975 and 1993, on all but the first occasion in search of salmon, but now most Norwegian rivers are closed to fishermen as the stocks have sunk to such a low level. However, my record books enable me to re-live many of the moments, both high and low, that occurred in that period of time.

I have already mentioned, in Chapter 2, how we first went on a car tour from Bergen in 1975 and came across the Voss river. I think the organiser of the Bolstad fishing when we first visited was a man called Haroldson who advertised his fishing with the words "Come to Norway and catch the fish of a lifetime". In those days there were a lot of salmon about and the Voss was one of the best rivers in Norway. How lucky can you get?

When we set out on our return trip in June 1975 we flew to Bergen and took the train to Bolstad where we were met by Haroldson and the ghillies who took the baggage while we walked up to the lodge. We were in time to have a meal before starting to fish at 10 p.m. I remember I was fishing opposite the lodge when at about 11 p.m. I heard a cry and saw a boat being pulled downstream by a fish being played by a fellow guest, a

Norway

Norwegian from Oslo who had, I remember, a goatee beard. He was in the stern of the boat, his rod was bent double and his beard accentuated the picture of concentration. As the boat passed through our beat my ghillie said we must go down to the fiord to see the fish landed, so off we went and arrived just in time to see the fish landed. It was huge! So imagine our surprise when, on looking into the boat we saw another fish of the same size already taken by the Norwegian. Both fish weighed in at 40 lbs. each. What a way to start a fishing holiday!

The next day I was in a boat in a pool called Rontgen with a ghillie who was a worker on the railway. He was about 50, had no English, but he knew every inch of the river. The method of fishing was to bounce a prawn across the bottom. If the prawn suddenly stopped it was either stuck in the rocks or, if it started moving, it was a fish! My experience of Norwegian fish is that if it was big (30 lbs. plus) it moved about the bottom very slowly to start with whereas a smaller fish would dash about immediately. Anyway, on this morning the bottom moved and I started playing my first Norwegian salmon. The river was quite high with a lot of white water between the pools and although I tried to keep the fish in the pool he decided to set off for the sea. We had to follow through the white water (it wasn't till later that I realised how big the waves were) to the next pool down where the ghillie beached the boat and gaffed the fish. And what a fish - 47 lbs.

The following morning Jane had the same ghillie in the same pool and she too hooked a fish which she managed to land without going through the white water. I was fishing the next pool down and the first I knew of this was when she appeared on the bank with a huge smirk on her face and told me, when I

Norway

asked, that it was 23 lbs.! Not bad for a first (and only) salmon. But in spite of this, as I've already pointed out, she never became a fisherman. Two more fish the next day making up the four averaging 30 lbs.

This trip whetted my appetite so the following year, 1976, the Bolstad being all booked up I went with David Lemon to the Sundane river, some 100 miles or so North of Bergen. We flew to Bergen and then boarded a small coaster that sailed overnight to Sundane. At that time of year, late May, it was light for most of the night and we called in at several villages to deliver and collect all sorts of goods - from livestock to machinery to food and mail. I think a lot of these villages were only accessible from the sea so they depended on the local boat to keep them supplied. We each had a bunk, quite rudimentary, but David was up and about most of the night overseeing the loading and unloading of the ship!

We arrived at 7.50 a.m. and were fishing by 10.30. The only fish caught that day was a 10.7 kilo salmon caught at 9.00 p.m. by a 78 year old Norwegian. Next day David lost one, the next day was blank as well but we were introduced to "Funeral Porridge" which consisted of prunes, apricots and raisins boiled together - I did not record the outcome but the name was bad enough! The following day I had a fish (16 lbs.) hooked at 8.10 a.m. on a Red Jensen Pirken and the very next day David had one (13 lbs.) hooked at 8.10 a.m. also on a Red Jensen Pirken. On these two days, between fishing, we visited a fox farm (not very nice) a fur factory, a ski jump and a furniture factory. I note we had a boozy party with Foxy (the owner of the fox farm), not very difficult in Norway as once they start drinking they make a day of it!

Norway

Another blank day followed so David, not really being a dedicated fisherman, got a bit bored so we decided to come home early. We cancelled our coaster berth, caught a little aeroplane from Sundane, landed in Bergen just in time to catch the S.A.S. plan for London and arrived at 5.45 - four and a half hours instead of twentyfour. So ended our Sundane adventure.

The following year, 1977, we returned to the Voss from 20 - 26 June, but this time a few miles upstream at Skorvelein. This was a private house owned by Col. Dian Beard together with the fishing. We flew to Bergen, hired a car and drove to Voss (town) and then down to the house just above Evanger. This was the first time we met Minto Wilson who was acting as the fishing manager for the Beards. The other guests were two English, two American and three Norwegians. We were surprised to see two English girl cooks, one of whom we knew as she had competed at one of our earlier Horse Trials at Rushall and was the daughter of the well known trainer, Dick Stillwell. Julia and her friend, Henrietta kept us very well fed for the whole week. Two of the ghillies were English lads, Patrick and Arthur.

Driving down from Voss lake to Evanger was new country to us so we were told to look out for a house, high above the river, flying the Union Jack. We espied the house up a very steep gravel drive with a sharp corner at the top. It took me two attempts to reach the top as we kept spinning on the corner. So we arrived to be greeted by the Beards, Minto and the rest of the staff. Thus began our long association with the Voss river and with Minto who we soon discovered knew every salmon river in England and Scotland together with most of the fishermen!

My diary of the week tells the story:

Norway

20 June Monday. To Evanger by car. Went out with Patrick on Beat 2. Split cane rod. Patrick said "I will show you how to cast here - no-one but a fool can get stuck on the bottom here". First cast - stuck on bottom. Yanked rod and broke it. Good start! Later hooked fish on Beat 1, towed it 600 yds. to island. Jane and Patrick got out and as fish came to gaff it fell off.

21 - 24 June. Very hot all week - water dropping whole time due to lack of snow in mountains last winter. Fish "coming short" all week. Seemed to be going for eyes and these heads were nipped out with no real takers. Food in "hotel" very good. Very nice atmosphere.

25 June. Saturday. Out at 6 a.m. - started fishing No.1 at 6.30. Cloudy for first time. Water down - about 18 inches over shelf. Prawn. Hooked fish 7.25 a.m. standing in little bay in shelf below Stanley's hat (a triangular rock that looked like a top hat). Three main runs - first after milling around in pool across river when I saw tail in shallower water. Then it came to bay, saw me and shot across river again. In again, thrashed about and then took off for rapids. Turned in V just above and got him back to bay. Gaffed him after about two final plunges - scrambled to shore, up embankment, stuffed him in a hole, knelt on him and gave his coup de grace. 55 lbs. 52" long. 28" girth. River life 3 years. Sea life 5 years. Maiden cock. Condition Factor 105.

How I carried him on my little gaff with one hand through 20 yards of rocky water I shall never know. When I came to carry him to the boat it was all I could do with both hands free with no rod or wading stick.

The one disappointment was this: all week I had been going out before breakfast - there was a heat wave - and when I came back, the rest of the party were usually at it. For the first three days they would all ask as I got in "Catch one?" I had to say "no". On the Thursday and Friday they didn't even bother to ask! One of the thoughts that went through my mind when I was playing the fish (and praying it wouldn't get off!) was how I would surprise them all at breakfast!

I planned to carry it to the house on my back, lay it in the hall and hope someone would trip over it when they came out from breakfast! However, one of the Norwegians in the house who couldn't sleep, got up early and happened to be looking down on the river while I was struggling to get the fish into the boat. He raised the alarm so instead of creeping up unseen I was met by the whole house party - clapping!

My week was made by our flight home from Bergen on S.A.S. There was an empty seat next to me and I wondered why. Just before take-off when the cabin crew were told to take their seats, my empty seat was taken by one of the prettiest girls it has ever been my pleasure to see! S.A.S. cabin crew were about to go on strike for some reason or other and I felt sure that such a pretty girl would not be joining them. Not a bit of it - she was right up there with the rest and said she would certainly be joining them. She certainly was a stunner!

Not all of our visits to Norway were successful as far as the fishing was concerned. In 1979 and 1981 we caught nothing. In 1979 the river was nine feet above normal, not because of rain as would be the case in England, but because of the sun. When they have a sudden heat-wave the snow on the glaciers melts and the rivers rise dramatically. Instead of dirty muddy water the rivers run absolutely clear and are really rather spectacular, although no good for fishing. 1988 and 1991 were also blank, the second being particularly disappointing as it was the first time I had persuaded Bob Browning to come with us. More of that later.

We took our son Stephen with us twice and he managed to catch a few fish, the best of 39.5 lbs. caught in Wookey Hole. In the course of fishing Skorve Osen I had discovered a spot, just below the island, where the fish seemed to lie. As you bounced your prawn along the bottom the river bed gradually sloped down for several yards and then started to rise quite quickly. You had to work the boat so that you crossed this area from shallow towards the deep and the fish would take as the prawn or shrimp started to rise. And you had to position the boat exactly in line with a railway hut on the bank. We caught several there, including this one of Stephen's which he caught in the pouring rain just before he had to catch a train back to Bergen and England. Minto, who always came up with special names for landmarks on the river decided to call this spot Wookey Hole but in later years he told people that it was an old discarded tractor tyre! Other names were Stanley's Hat, already mentioned, and Banbury. This was a fish that rose regularly in the very centre of the Skorve lake and when asked why he called it Banbury he said it was because Banbury was in the very centre of England. Incidentally, Banbury was never caught!

One evening, as Minto was a bit of a disbeliever about Wookey Hole, I said I would take him out and show him where it was. As the sun sets very late I insisted that we should not start fishing until 10 p.m. and while waiting we were sitting on the edge of the railway line that follows the river very closely at

Norway

Skorve. We were chatting away and didn't hear the Oslo express approaching from the Bergen direction, until it was very near us when we scrambled down the bank but not before the driver had seen us and slammed on his brakes. Not only did he stop, he also climbed down from the engine and started berating us in fluent Norwegian. Somehow or other Minto managed to placate him, he got into his cab and continued on his way to Oslo. The railway all along this stretch is single track and it must have been a great engineering feat to build it in that mountainous countryside.

But back to our fishing - at 10 p.m. I rowed out to Wookey Hole, told Minto where to cast and at the critical point he hooked a fish - 20 lbs. It was then his turn to row and we covered the same spot and I had one - another 20 lbs. And we were back in the house by 11 p.m. Not a bad evening's work!

There was a very large pool at the top end of the Skorve fishing that was somehow shared with the locals but which we fished on odd days. It is called Ho, a very small name for a very large pool - at least two acres if one can describe water in acres. It is also somewhat sinister as it is very deep and is surrounded by trees and gives the impression that it must be full of fish. We did catch a few there but there are four things that make it stand out in my memory. The first concerns the railway that runs along the far bank and at one point, as can be seen from the sketch, it is very close. Evidently when the original owner of the Skorve fishing was in residence and wanted to fish in Ho he arranged for the train to stop at a Halt he had constructed there so that he could fish it! I think he was an Englishman, possibly a parson, as at that time the Norwegians had not embraced salmon fishing with rod and line - they used horizontal nets set out

Norway

where the salmon crossed a shallower area on their journey upriver. This net was held in place by ropes that ran over a pulley fixed in a tree and attached to a large weight - rock. A short length of rope held the weight in place and the fisherman, sitting on a platform in the tree, would have a sharp knife and when he saw a salmon crossing his net he would cut the restraining rope, the rock would drop and the net would encircle the fish. Old-fashioned but, I'm told, very effective when there were a lot of salmon running, but the younger Norwegians find it too boring so they let their fishing to mad Englishmen and work in the towns!

The next occasion was when I took Jane to fish there in 1983 and we were fishing the Aspen Lie when she hooked a fish. We were near the bank where there were a lot of big rocks in the water and I tried to beach the boat but the fish kept getting around the rocks and after about ten minutes he "broke" her. Now this is why I remember this incident so vividly. As every fisherman knows, when you get broken on a rock there is a clean break. When one of your knots comes undone you are left with a tell-tale curl like a pig's tail. On this occasion Jane thought the fish had broken her on a rock, but when I examined the line I found a pig's tail - one of my knots had failed. I never let on as I was too ashamed to acknowledge that she had lost her fish because of my bad knot and, until she reads this, she will still think it was a sharp rock! When discussing this with Minto (I didn't tell him about the knot!) he told me that I should have moved the boat to the other side of the river where there is a sandy beach to make landing a fish easy. Another mistake!

The third occasion that sticks in my mind was one afternoon when Minto and I went plumbing. There was a seriously big fish

Norway

lying just off the rock garden that would taunt us about once an hour by rising and showing himself. We tried fishing for him to no avail so we decided to see if we could find his hiding place by sounding the bottom with a large weight. All we really discovered was that it was all very deep in that particular area so we didn't achieve much. The fish was never caught to our knowledge so I'm not sure how big it was but my estimate at the time was that he could well have been 60 lbs. - he really looked enormous when we saw him move.

And the last incident was pure comic opera! Stephen and Jane were going to Voss to take a fish for smoking so they agreed to drop me at Ho while they went to deliver the fish. They would call in and collect me on their way home. I took the best boat (there were only two) and went to the spot marked X, anchored and started fishing where we had seen a fish rise earlier in the day. I hooked him after about half and hour and started playing him. I have never hooked and landed a big fish in a boat by myself and always thought that I would cross that bridge when I got to it. Well, I got to it that afternoon and after a few minutes while we (the fish and I) were sizing things up I began to wonder how I was going to get him into the boat. I had my small gaff but not being expert in boat fishing alone, everytime I leaned over the side the boat threatened to capsize. I tried in the stern but the fish had other ideas and I was conscious all the time that the anchor rope was lurking in the water. So, after about half an hour, we arrived at a stalemate - I couldn't gaff him from the boat and I couldn't pull up the anchor, row the boat and play the fish all at the same time.

This was where the comic opera starts. There was I, in mid-river, anchored, with a big fish milling around the boat, with no

Norway

idea what to do. At that very moment, Jane and Stephen called in to pick me up on their way back from Voss. As they came out of the trees by the boats I heard Stephen say "He's got a fish", Jane said "Has he?" and Stephen said "Yes, he has". Then began a somewhat hectic conversation between me in the boat and them on the bank. All sorts of advice was offered - "Gaff him", "Row to the shore", "Cut the line," "Let him go", and most useful of all, "We can't wait here all night." By this time things were getting a bit fraught so Stephen decided to take the other boat, a very small and unseaworthy affair, and row out with Jane to help me. As they approached my boat the fish got a bit excited so I shouted to them to keep their distance, only to be met with "How can we help you if you won't let us near you?" This went on for a bit when we all decided we must do something. The something was for Stephen to row his boat upstream of my boat and then for Jane to grab my anchor rope, pull up the anchor, put it in their boat and for Stephen then to tow us ashore. For some reason he rowed to the far shore which was a bit rocky instead of to the boat landing where there was a shelving beach. He reached the bank, got out and pulled my boat in close. Then we had to gaff the fish amid the boats. I asked Stephen if he had ever gaffed a fish before and he said "No." So then I started issuing a stream of quite possibly contradictory instructions while Jane looked on and offered further advice. Eventually Stephen gaffed his first fish very successfully - and I had a lovely 30 lber!

One of the best fish caught during my stays in Norway was on the 18th June 1987. One of the guests, Peter Fraser, went out before breakfast by himself to fish the pool known as Langhul - a wide stretch of the river, about six foot deep with a nice flow.

He was fishing a fly and came back to breakfast carrying a 42 lb. fish!

Another fisherman, David Thompson, had a memorable week in June 1990. On his first day he hooked a fish and he had with him the head Norwegian ghillie, Leidulf. After a minute or so Leidulf said "I think it is a small trout." After another twenty minutes he said "I think he is growing". By the time he was landed he had grown to 22 lbs! That was by way of being the overture. On June 21st he had another fish, this time hooked in the Evanger lake Osen, the top beat of the Bolstad fishing. He landed it in the fiord after coming all the way down the river in two hours 24 minutes! Briefly, the story was - he and his ghillie spotted the fish lying near the bank at the tail of Evanger Lake. They tried everything - prawns, shrimps, spinners etc. and couldn't interest him in anything so they tried a fly and he took it! When fishing the Evanger Lake Osen it was essential to try and keep a fish in the lake and above the bridge that crosses the river at this point. Otherwise, you are into very fast water where there is usually a standing wave of about four feet - rather frightening. Added to which, the boat in use in the lake was one of the smaller variety and not very stable. After about half an hour the fish decided he'd had enough of the lake and headed downstream. Then there was nothing they could do but follow. By this time Minto had arrived and decided it wasn't safe for them to continue in the small boat so he called them in to the next boat station and made them change into a larger, more stable boat. This gave the fish a breathing space so when they tried to bring him in he set off down-stream again. We, the rest of the party, were in the lodge having supper when Minto rang to say that David was into a big one and was heading in our direction. Jane and I dashed out (the Americans stayed put eating their dinner!), grabbed a car and motored up to meet the boat. At just this moment, David had got his line fouled round a fence post sticking out of the water and was shouting for help. Two of the Norwegian ghillies jumped into a boat and started rowing across to see if they could free the line, but by the time they were half-way across the line became free - and off they went down river again. There is another bridge at the bottom of the beat and we drove down to see them pass. What struck me was the colour of David's face! He was as white as a sheet and looked really worried. No wonder, because by now he had had the fish on for about two hours. Anyway, they shot under the bridge, negotiated the rapids above the fiord and brought the boat into the landing area. The ghillie got out with his gaff only for the fish to take off again. He went right across the fiord - at that point about 200 yards wide - with the boat in close attendance and then allowed them to tow him back again. The ghillie gaffed him after 2 hours. 24 minutes and he weighed in at 35 lbs. A truly memorable fish.

The only sad thing was that when Jane asked him to ring his wife back in England and tell her of his epic, he said "No. She wouldn't be interested."

Before leaving Norway I must mention the ghillie, Kaare, I had at Bolstad. He was a local farmer's son who lived way up in the mountains and when I first met him he only had three words of English which is why, I think, Minto put him with me. Not that I had any Norwegian - in fact, I knew only one word "Laks" which means salmon! - but I had fished in Norway before so he felt we might get on together being a farmer's son myself. His three words, which he used on many occasions when I was

Norway

casting, were "One metre more". So if he wanted me to cast six metres more he had to repeat "one metre more" six times until he was satisfied. He knew the river like the back of his hand and we spent many happy hours together - and caught quite a few fish.

Kaare with a fish from the bridge pool

Norway

The only snag with Kaare was that he would occasionally go a.w.o.l. and these absences would always be the result of a party the previous night. There was a Scottish ghillie from the Tweed at Bolstad at that time and he and Kaare were deadly when they started drinking! I think they must have each been trying to uphold their national pride! On one occasion Kaare was absent for several days and it transpired that on his way back from the local village he had been involved in an accident so he had taken to the hills to avoid being arrested. The fixed penalty for drink driving in Norway was (and perhaps still is) three weeks in prison. The only consolation was that you could choose the timing of your visit to jail - perhaps to coincide with your annual holiday so that your bosses might never know you had been to prison.

There are many memories of catching fish with Kaare (pronounced as Cora) but the incident I recall particularly was when he wasn't there! The day before he had been teaching me how to fish a certain pool which consisted of a fair current coming from the far side diagonally towards my bank. The trick was to drop your prawn on the edge of the current and let it bounce round until it reached your bank and began straightening out. You had to be very accurate and we had a lot of "one metre mores" before I got it right. Next morning I went out early by myself and tried to do what Kaare had taught me. My diary says "Copybook Kaare" as I went home with a 20 lber from just where he told me to fish. He was a great ghillie.

Chapter 8

ROGER'S PIKE

The story starts back in the early Spring (of 1996) when Roger and his daughter were looking into the river at Sheep Bridge. Suddenly Roger saw a very big fish cruising slowly upstream. He pointed it out to his daughter and they both agreed it must be a pike - so big that it seemed to fill the whole river. It turned and retreated downstream so when Roger reported it to me we decided to bait for it in the pools in Charlton Withy bed. I caught some small rainbows from the river at Upavon and set up some dead baits but all to no avail. When they were rotten we gave up and I began to wonder if perhaps Roger had been exaggerating!

In early June, Bob Walters was fishing off the footbridge opposite France Pond. He was casting for a trout that was rising near the bank when he saw a very large fish cruising very slowly upstream. It went under the bridge in a channel in the lily pad and suddenly exploded, took his fish and came back downstream right underneath him. He thought it marvellous - to see a pike take a trout. I thought it horrific - how many had he taken and how many more would he take. His estimate of its size was very large.

I took my spinning rod over and fished the area below the footbridge to no avail except that I thought I moved a big fish once - I saw a yellow flash in the water but no contact. We then made a pike trap and placed it under the footbridge in the channel where he had been seen, baited it with tasty fish and hoped. Nothing.

All went quiet for a week or so until Philip Vickers saw him again. This time it was cruising in the backwater behind the island at France and he had every chance to see it very clearly. Apart from being a very big pike, he told me that it had a white mark on its near-side flank, triangular in shape. I told Roger who next day found this fish - lying right under the bank on the far side of the backwater. He was facing downstream - there is no flow in the backwater and it took me some time to pick him out as I was looking for his head the opposite end! Roger said he thought he was facing downstream so we looked for Philip's white mark which would be visible if he was facing downstream. Sure enough, we saw it and then the whole outline became apparent - a huge pike lying right under some bushes on the opposite bank and only, seemingly, an inch or so under water.

There was only one thing to do - get the gun. So I rushed home and collected my 20 bore and a few cartridges (just in case!) and re-joined Roger on the island. We had some discussion on where to shoot - we had both heard that you have to shoot under a fish lying in the water - and eventually decided I should shoot about 6 inches under the fish. It seemed odd deliberately to shoot where the fish was not but I did try and depress the gun - and fired. A huge splash as the shot hit the water, a huge commotion as the pike dashed out into the middle of the backwater and another shot to make sure. This seemed only to persuade the pike he was persona non grata so he took off like a torpedo towards the hatches and we lost him. But with two shots

Roger's Pike

at point blank range we felt he must surely die and we would wait for his corpse to surface.

We waited - nothing emerged. We decided he must be trapped, dead under the roots of some alders as he had not been seen, and felt satisfied we had dealt with him.

One morning in early July, Nigel rang to say he had seen a pike and it was lying about 50 yards below the footbridge in among the lily pads. I collected my gun and rod, took Tajo (our gardener) and a gaff and felt certain we would get him this time. When we joined Nigel on the bank and he showed us the fish we had a bit of a discussion as to whether to shoot it or hook it. Eventually, as he was so near the surface we decided to shoot it so the same problem arose - where to shoot? It was huge - like a submarine quite impossible to miss so I shot at it. Boom! Another huge commotion in the water and the fish shot to the surface and we all said "Got him", whereupon he righted himself and swam away! I was so certain he was hit that I didn't give him the second barrel when he was on the surface - I just let him go! Was I cross?!

Next day, Tajo and I were cutting the lilies below the footbridge when we must have got rather too near him for comfort as the pike suddenly decided to clear off and made a terrific wake as he went downstream. Evidently he didn't feel too inconvenienced by my shooting! The following day Roger saw him and tried to harpoon him but missed.

A week or so later I had another 'phone call from Nigel saying the fish was lying just below the Church bridge. By the time I got there his children had been to have a look and had scared him off. However, that evening he was back so I went over with my snatcher - a large treble on my spinning rod as I had given up all hope of shooting it. He was lying absolutely still close to the southern downstream abutment - an easy place to snitch. I lowered the hook beside him to the left and with a mighty swish to the right expected the hook to connect. Instead, the hook flew up into a tree and got stuck! I just couldn't believe I had missed him - he was so big and so still that I just couldn't miss - but miss him I had and I was mad.

Just then Roger turned up to see if he could find the pike. I explained what I'd tried to do and said I expected the pike had vanished. We all peered in, Nigel, his gardener Ralph, Roger and I, the pike was still there, just in the same place. I had not even frightened him! So I told Roger he must have a go with his harpoon.

I should explain that some years ago we had a pike in France Pond. How it got there we don't know but by the time he was seen he was 8 lbs. I tried spinning for it, I tried to shoot it but never saw it so Roger made himself a harpoon. Made out of an old hay tedder tine, it had a wicked point and a substantial barb and fitted onto the end of a long pole. The idea was to stab the pike when the harpoon would come free from the pole and the fish could be pulled in with the cord attached to the base of the harpoon. One day Roger had his chance. He saw the fish near the surface but too far out to stab so he had to throw the harpoon. He hit the fish but in his struggle he came free and disappeared. However, a few days later his corpse surfaced - Roger had got his pike!

Roger assembled his harpoon on the bridge, got right above it and stabbed. Another huge commotion - and again the pike came off and disappeared. Now there were two disappointed pike catchers - Roger and I, but Roger had at least made contact

Roger's Pike

and he was quite sure that "that pike would never take another trout." We all went home hoping he was right.

Next morning I had another 'phone call - "Roger has got the pike." He had it in his car and was bringing it over to show me and to get it weighed - no one had scales big enough to cope with it!

What happened was this - Roger had gone down the next morning and had seen the pike lying upstream of the bridge, half in and half out of the lily pad. As he watched it moved gradually downstream a foot or so to be clear of the lilies and had then moved up again. It was too far upstream of the bridge for Roger to stab it so he decided to throw his harpoon - there was no other way. So he threw it from the bridge - and missed, but the pike didn't move. So he threw it again - and missed again. After some thought he decided to try and throw the harpoon from the Church end of the bridge and try and hit the pike sideways instead of in the back - a longer throw but a bigger target. This time he was successful - the harpoon found its mark and stayed in but the handle also stayed connected to the harpoon instead of coming free. Roger still had the cord in his hand and managed to manoeuvre the fish into the (Church) side of the river onto the roots of the alder growing there. Then he was stuck - he couldn't climb down to the fish, the handle was lying in the water and he had the gaff in his pocket (with no handle as he used the same handle for both gaff and harpoon). So he decided to lower the gaff to hook up the handle so he could try and remove the harpoon and replace it with the gaff to deal with the fish. Just as he was about to do this the fish struggled, came free of the harpoon and started wallowing in the centre of the river. It was in a pretty bad state by this time so Roger quickly drew up the

Roger's Pike

harpoon and handle with the cord, replaced the harpoon with the gaff and as the fish gradually fell back downstream under the bridge he managed to gaff it and lift it over the parapet onto the road.

The pike weighed 16 lbs. and in his throat was a 12oz. trout!

Roger with his 16 lb monster – and harpoon

Roger's Pike

Roger English was the retired keeper at Rushall who kept an eye on the fishing after his retirement.

Co-incidentally, he was Charles Ashton's driver during the war. They both joined the 2nd. Field Regiment, RA at the same time in 1939, Roger as an under-age gunner and Charles as a newly commissioned 2nd. Lieutenant. They were together from Dunkirk until 1941 and did not meet again until the 1960's when there was a skittles match between the Tedworth Hunt and the local keepers. Roger evidently asked a fellow keeper who lived in Milton (Charles' village) if "that man over there was Major Charlie Ashton". When told he was Roger asked "Can he still cuss?". There is no record of the answer!

Chapter 9

HORSES AND HUNTING

My hunting exploits have not been of the vintage variety. To start with, most of my hunting has been with the Tedworth whose country is renowned as being a difficult scenting one. This is not to say we didn't have a lot of fun, especially earlier when we had several hunting farmers out and we probably misbehaved as young men usually do! Strangely, the best scenting was often on the Larkhill Ranges which became known as the cream of the shell-hole country! When a fox ran along a track made by a tank it always seemed to carry a good scent and we had some good runs. Perhaps the days I remember best were Boxing Days. We would always hack to the meet in Pewsey and over the years we developed a good "route of good cheer!". The first port of call was to the Fergusons at Manningford who were always very generous with the port, even to the extent of leaving a decanter and glasses on a stone in their drive if they were away. Next stop the Phoenix in Pewsey, now no longer a pub but a very tasteful development of town houses. Then to the Meet outside the old cinema where there was always some kind soul with a bottle! Hounds always drew Jones' Mill first which gave me the opportunity to visit the Peall Crosses at Milk House Water where I would sample their home-made sloe gin whilst their daughter would borrow my hat, hop onto my horse and,

Horses and Hunting

much to the consternation of her mother, go off after the field for a few minutes. After being re-united we called in to the Campions who always seemed to have some very good mince pies left over from Christmas - not to mention a tot or two as well! Then up to Everleigh Ashes and to Jack Mayall's house. Jack only knew how to pour whiskey by the tumbler full so my memories after that visit are somewhat hazy. Eventually we would hack back home via R.A.F. Upavon where on one occasion I was on my own and there was a good party going on in one of the quarters. By now it was about four o'clock and the master of the house came running out with a huge glass of whiskey which he insisted I drank with him - which I did! Luckily I was on my old hunter, Topper, who knew his way home where we arrived in a drunken haze!

Setting out for a Boxing Day Meet

Horses and Hunting

While Charles Ashton was still riding I went down to hunt with the New Forest on several occasions. Charles had a small horse of about 15 hands, so could happily gallop through the trees but on my horse it was not so easy as the forest ponies could not reach up high enough to browse on the higher branches. But it was a lovely place to see hounds at work. On 22 March 1969 Charles and I went to their meet at Bratley Woods hoping to watch his friend Sir Newton Rycroft hunting hounds. Sadly, on that particular day he was confined to bed with the 'flu', so the horn was being carried by the kennel-huntsman, Harry. There was a thin east wind and no scent and the hounds soon got bored and started looking for their "Master". As they emerged from one of the newly-planted forestry blocks they gradually formed themselves into a group, sat on their haunches and started howling. I see in my diary that I called it the "Newton Lament", and we all felt very sorry for Harry - evidently the New Forest hounds were at that time very much a one man pack. We did find eventually at 2.30 p.m. and had a good hunt but sadly Harry got lost! Not his day!

Earlier in the day, before the actual Meet, I saw something I had not seen before or since. There was a block of "daddy" heather (tall old heather) being cut with a grass cutter which was followed by a baler baling it. I asked some locals why the heather was being baled and they told me that it was used as a base for building a road on soft ground as it never rots. Later I was told it was used in the foundations of Salisbury Cathedral for the same reason, but I never had that confirmed although I can quite understand that it never rots as it is like spring steel when old.

Horses and Hunting

**With the Warwickshire
R to L Peter Horton, Bill Hobbs, B.W.**

For the record, I hunted occasionally with other packs of hounds - the Avon Vale, R.A. Salisbury Plain, Craven, Beaufort, V.W.H. Old Berks, Heythrop, Warwickshire (already mentioned) and once with the Cheshire Hunt in the U.S. of A. This last, which I have also followed on foot or in a car, was remarkable in that they never wanted to kill their fox! They were quite happy (as I suspect most followers are in England) to have a good run and then to wish their fox goodbye until the next time. They seemed to be quite sad when the hunt ended with a kill as they wanted their fox for the rest of the season! Perhaps we could take a leaf out of their book and call it "fox exercise" to make sure the fox was fit and well - as opposed to "hound exercise" which might go wrong if a fox jumps up in front of hounds. "We were not trying to kill the fox, Your Worship, we were just ensuring that it keeps fit!" This might go down well with a Bench from the country but I doubt if the urbanites who enacted the recent Anti-Hunting Bill would appreciate it!

Not being a brave rider I was often apprehensive out hunting when faced with a big obstacle - open ditches were the most dreaded as I was always expecting to finish up in the bottom with the horse on top of me. This happened to me once and scared as I was it was as nothing to the fear we used to experience when taken hunting in her car by a relation of our daughter Caroline who lives in America. The driver of the car was the mother of Caroline's brother-in-law and the last time she took us hunting she must have been in her late eighties. She had lived her life in the area, had hunted all her life and knew every byway and track in the district. This was fine until they found a fox when her excitement became so great that such things as the rules of the road were completely forgotten! She would drive at speed wherever she went, would turn across the road or reverse back up a road - anything to keep hounds in view - her enthusiasm was so infectious we found ourselves urging her on! But we were glad when we adjourned for lunch in the local pub - always clam chowder.

From 1962 to 1972 I had the honour (?!) of being the D.C. of the Tedworth Pony Club and this really began our greater interest in the horse world.

Starting the young!

We started with rallies on the farm and ended up with the Area Eventing Final - which led Lord Hugh Russell into persuading us to run a Novice Horse Trial. This we did from 1970 - 1985 by which time we had added Intermediate and Advanced Classes. The following account of the 1979 Rushall Horse Trials, written by Jane for the Midland Bank Handbook sums up very well the trials and tribulations of Event Organisers. Perhaps I should add that the Midland Bank generously sponsored nearly all Horse Trials, including ours, for the whole time we ran - they were very good to us and to Eventing in general and I would like to record our sincere thanks to them here.

'...and it was still raining'

by Jane Wookey

Barry and I had decided that this year was to be the best Rushall ever. After two successive years when we had been on the point of cancelling, the law of averages must ensure that we were due for a fine day. At their final meeting the Committee had agreed that insurance was unnecessary. The premiums were too high, and so much repair work had been done to the course in 1978 that we should be able to run in virtually any conditions that an English spring could produce.

The omens were all good. Despite Barry's concern that too much fence sponsoring would reduce the impact of Midland Bank, it was obvious that this was a concession we would have to make after a heavy financial loss the previous year. The response to his appeal was most encouraging, both from small local firms and the larger business interests. Applications for trade stands were greater than they had ever been and we were full of optimism. The only early setback was the news that Salisbury Racecourse would not be available for stabling owing to quarantine regulations affecting a race meeting the following week. This arrangement with Salisbury had suited us perfectly in the past, as the Stable Manager had taken over all bookings, payments, and the inevitable last-minute alterations with no reference to us whatsoever. However, the Army at Tidworth and Larkhill generously agreed to provide the necessary boxes - we simply had to sort out the demand.

On 21 February the first batch of entries arrived, apart from a few which had jumped the gun and which were immediately followed by apologetic telephone calls. This is the one part of the Horse Trials that I really enjoy. It is all anticipation and, as yet, no real anxiety. We have a systematic procedure at the end of breakfast every morning: Barry insists on opening each envelope meticulously with his paper-knife, just to satisfy his curiosity, and then I check each one for the correct entry money, cheque signature, class and whether it carries a priority stamp. The entry is then returned to the envelope, on which the details are recorded. Thus we keep a 'state of the poll' from day to day. The entries this year were higher than ever and full of interest. We recognized the names of several of the riders we had seen at Lexington, and a number of other foreign competitors.

The first real problem arose on ballot day. Up to then the 450 entries seemed a cause for satisfaction, perhaps even flattering, but sooner or later the fact had to be faced that it was only possible to run a certain number of horses in one day without creating chaos. Barry, as the timing expert, reckoned we could afford to run one extra Novice Section without extending the day too much. Basing the classes as accurately as possible on the demand, left us with 1 Advanced, 2 Intermediate and 4 Novice sections. Bearing in mind that the rate of fall-out for one reason or another is highest at Advanced level, and that, in any case, their dressage was to be run on two days, we decided to accept 60 in that class, 90 Intermediates and 166 Novices. This meant refusing about 140 entries. The Advanced and Intermediate were straightforward - priorities only - which at least made that task an easy one. In the Novices we balloted for twenty non-priorities. Once the final decision is made it must be binding, except in a very rare case where perhaps a priority stamp for some good reason has been delayed. Otherwise as an Organizer you are in for trouble! No matter how many pleading and undoubtedly genuine telephone calls we have (and this year there were more than ever), it is impossible for us to decide the most deserving cases. We do at least make a real effort to inform unsuccessful applicants by the first available post, if that is any consolation.

Once we have accepted the entries they are all sorted into alphabetical order of classes, for quick reference, and then recorded on a vast master sheet, which Barry complains is a waste of time, but to which I refer constantly. Then we have a few days of comparative peace, apart from the telephone, until entries close.

This year, by 9 March the pace had begun to increase considerably. Worries about the weather were setting in. Very little drilling could be done, so the farm men were busy preparing dressage arenas, marking areas for trade stands, making ready the show jumping ring, plumbing the loos, as well as a vast amount of roping and endless other jobs. It already seemed probable that we should have to move the car park up on the hill. Extra hardcore was laid at each of the entrances, but even so we were still convinced that the weather would improve.

In the house the daunting task of sorting out entries into sections began. Three-horse riders, who rarely ride more than two when the time comes, two-horse riders, and those with a long distance to travel do not consider a 9am dressage convenient. This year the Intermediates inevitably had a very prolonged day, and in some cases we were able to fit a second horse into the gap between dressage and show jumping. Invariably we make some mistakes, but they are unintentional. At last the lists were complete and we started on the seemingly endless job of sending out details to each competitor. How we cherish those who have filled in their entry forms legibly and accurately! Marilyn, Barry's farm secretary, is invaluable on these occasions and is continually being dispatched to the typewriter. The printers were our next concern. They had to be given the details at once, to enable us to check and return the proofs for the completed programme. The introductory pages had already been proofed and had passed Barry's careful scrutiny.

From that moment the telephone never seemed to stop. Several competitors forgot to mention that they were not available for Friday dressage! Requests for special passes, details for the press, stabling problems, withdrawals - but far too few. What would happen if we were left with 300 horses on 31 March, and it was still raining? We were almost greeting withdrawals with a sigh of relief. The cardinal rule which must never be forgotten at this time is that every 'phone call is written down immediately. Crookham had an unbelievably ghastly weekend, and had to cancel. Frantic phone calls to Minto Wilson at Shelswell in case he should be obliged to follow suit - and still far too many horses. The rosettes had been ordered weeks before but had we checked to see that they were correct? Two trophies were being repaired, and one still had not been returned. Marilyn and I had agreed that our previous caterer had been none too happy in his work and so had opted for an enterprising alternative from Devon, which caused Barry much apprehension! It could well snow on 31 March in this year of grace. At this late stage should we try insurance after all? On inquiry, - yes we could. However, for the maximum of £1000 the premium would be £500.

Exactly a week before 'D Day' Barry arrived home in the evening with the comment that Stan, our farm handyman, had noticed a continual queue outside the 'ladies' loo the previous year, despite the conspicuous lack of spectators. Why hadn't we thought of that before? We had to have another 'ladies' within a week. When in doubt try the BHS. We caught Peter Hodgson just before the office closed. Phone Mrs. Tony Wootton, said he. She knows all about the arrangements at Tidworth. Larkhill had exactly what we required on hire for only £8, but that was already booked. We suddenly remembered a very efficient model that we had seen at Lockerley the previous year, but according to Gina Edmund's latest brochure the hire charge was now £60 per cubicle! Undeterred as ever, Barry set off with Stan first thing on Monday morning to a dealer near Andover who sells surplus Army and Navy equipment, and he returned with a magnificent R. N. trailer, already fitted with twenty-one electric power points and strip-lighting. Stan and Martin, our carpenter converted this within three days - to provide four cubicles and a wash basin, and it was a source of great pride to them.

Horses and Hunting

This same Monday with only five days to go, Badger, Barry's assistant course builder, course repairer, general factotum and expert on the Rushall cross-country, contracted the 'flu - and it was *still* raining.

By Tuesday evening, Barry was considering an emergency plan, so we drove up the hill behind the drier to see whether it was possible to move the dressage arenas and show jumping to the high ground. We were both surprised to find how much flat space was available. Our spirits lifted and completely new plans were put into operation the next morning. Sheets of instructions and information on the new layout were reproduced, to be handed to each competitor on arrival. By Thursday evening we had recorded 6.25 inches of rain for the month. With all the last-minute alterations we almost forgot to take the time sheets for the Friday dressage competitors over to Jenny Fry, the Rushall Manager's wife, who sits by the telephone for two successive evenings. By then Barry was beginning to have second thoughts.

The Friday of the trials, to me at any rate, is always the worst day. At this stage we are entirely committed, no going back, and all the expenses incurred. On this occasion, at least the appalling weather had meant cancellation of the large marquee and thus a considerable saving. All the secretarial side, scoreboards and bar were moved into the grain drier, and only two small solitary tents remained in the main field - one for the cross-country time-keepers and one for the scorers, who were immovable, thanks to our telephone scoring system. A group of Signallers had done a magnificent job that week, checking the lines to each fence, to the commentator, the dressage arenas, show jumping and cross-country. Within the last forty-eight hours they laid separate lines

Horses and Hunting

to the new venues and made good use of the local Post Office telephone poles.

"er, HELP! please"

RUSHALL'S UNIQUE TELEPHONE SYSTEM

On Friday morning Gina arrived at ten bringing an air of calm unflappability to our frayed nerves and proved to us once again how easy it is to work out an effective timing schedule if you can only remember how to start. The lists were complete by noon, when they were due to be taken to Pewsey for duplicating, just as the dressage judges arrived for pre-luncheon drinks. Immense relief at the sight of a volunteer to deliver the time sheets, but unfortunately he did not appreciate the urgency and disappeared for a three hour lunchbreak first. Lunch at the local pub for the dressage officials. I hardly dared to look at Colonel ffrench Blake, knowing we still had fifty-three Advanced horses, but at least it hadn't rained for twelve hours. Marilyn and Jan, our girl groom, were busy working out a running order from the time sheets while eating a picnic lunch, and Karen, who also comes to help in the Secretary's box, was handing out numbers at the drier. The afternoon went reasonably smoothly. Badger had recovered and it wasn't raining. But there were two missing dressage competitors in the Advanced class, both from Talland, and both had been seen walking the course. Could their communication system have broken down? At the sight of Gerry Sinnott's and Marina Scioccetti's faces when they realised their mistake, it was obvious that it had. And the Italian team trainer was flying over for the express purpose of watching Miss Scioccetti's performance! It couldn't have been her day, for later in the afternoon she was to be found with Anna Casagrande sitting disconsolately outside the dryer. The Talland crowd had gone home without them!

. We were able to relax in the evening when the dressage was over and we all foregathered in France Barn for a drink after the jump judges' briefing. There was an air of inevitability and general amazement that we were still struggling on. Barry and I were strongly aware of how extremely good-natured, long-suffering, generous and obliging all these people were. Most of them support us year after year and it is impossible to thank them adequately. Anyway, the alcohol helped and I returned home to find younger son Stephen eating bread and jam by an unlit fire, and chatting up the two Italian girls. Marina's luck was in as there had been two late withdrawals, who were due to do their dressage on Saturday and at last she produced a smile.

All was well until 7.40 on Saturday morning. As Karen and I were about to leave the house the caterers rang - their van wouldn't start! They had been working on it until midnight. Why

Horses and Hunting

not *all night* I couldn't help thinking. Panic set in. Karen thought I was going to have hysterics. My mind went quite blank. Sixty official lunches and all the usual catering. She had to leave to deal with early competitors with strict instructions not to say a word to Barry. I rang two neighbours who promised to go to Devizes to buy supplies. The bake house at the drier was organised to make bread and rolls, but little did David and Sue Fuller realise what they were going to have to contend with. I went over to Rushall with only a vague idea as to how we could possibly cope, and the 'phone rang in the drier almost immediately. The local publican's wife wanted to know if she could help and Barry overheard the conversation! Why couldn't we ask the two pubs to provide half the official lunches each? It had never entered my head. No problems! The stores arrived from Devizes, plus an offer of help from one of the shoppers, who disappeared into the 90 degrees of our bake house to help pack and hand out cheese, pate, pork pie and freshly-baked rolls and bread. We released Jan from her secretarial duties to relieve the pressure, as the demand for food was constant.

Looking back it is impossible to recall the day in detail. It is a blurred confusion of isolated incidents. Two loose dogs and

Horses and Hunting

Barry's announcement that they could be collected from the Secretary's for a fine of £20. Sue Hatherly turned up to claim one, with a rather worried grin - was the fine meant seriously? Barry said no, but he would collect if she won a prize. No one seemed to think that the other funny friendly little white terrier with a long back and short legs was worth £20, so we tied him up in the drier office. A phone call from home to say that the caterers were on their way after all. What on earth could I say to them if they arrived in time? Another harassed call from the dressage steward, Joyce Hayward. They were short of Intermediate dressage sheets. For the first time ever they had left the names to be filled in by the writers and had suddenly discovered that the ample supply of pink sheets were not all for the same test. Barry rushed Marilyn back home to the typewriter once again. They returned remarkably quickly, only to find that Stan, at that time controlling the parking at the drier, was needed urgently to repair a blocked pipe, so all 6 stone of Marilyn took over as car park attendant.

Horses and Hunting

Barry called in and asked if I'd like a quick trip on the cross-country. Karen seemed fine, and Marilyn was back from controlling the traffic, so I guiltily slipped away. So far the course was riding well. A few quick words with brother Thomas, standing on France Bridge and politely lifting his cap as each competitor shot by: 'Careful, bridge is slippery' and invariably receiving a hurried thank you in return.

An offer of some rather revolting coffee from son Nigel's double-decker bus, where he was feeding the baby and his wife was peeling sprouts and roasting pheasant. Surely this, at least, must be unique for a horse trial? A hasty visit to the thatched pavilion where Morris Nicoll looks after the doctors and vets. He was bored, thank heaven. Back to work, and no one had yet claimed the terrier. The announcer felt that he needed a walk. Barry arrived with armfuls of sweets presented by a grateful trade stand. The terrier was the only one who appreciated the coconut-covered mushrooms. Someone wished to see me, I was told. A smartly dressed young country gentleman approached. 'Special Branch' he whispered in my ear, and I felt terribly important. By now there was a colossal din in the drier. The bar was going full swing and everybody was shouting. The score-board writers were finding it very difficult to hear Gina's voice from the score tent. It was past midday and it still wasn't raining. For some extraordinary reason I was suddenly presented with two pages of show jumping scores, expressly intended for me I was told. John Wallis, one of the commentators, was at hand and said he needed them in the commentary box, so I gave them to him with the explicit instruction to check with the scorers first. He overlooked this minor detail, while the scorers were madly ringing and dashing in all directions to locate them. And for once the show jumping officials had omitted to use their carbons! I noticed the cherry brandy tucked in a corner. Who could we spare to dispense the customary cheer to the jump judges?

At periodic intervals Ian and Chris emerged from the bake house in a state of exhaustion. David and Sue Fuller had been baking for hours, and must have been more accustomed to the heat. My versatile co-secretary agreed to take over as relief. At least she would have had an interesting day. The VIPs were pleased with their lunches at the respective pubs, and the caterers turned up at 2.30pm. I hoped that they would manage to cover some of their expenses. Novice prize-giving was announced and no Midland Bank to be seen. Mrs. Boreham was there but where was the money?

All was well and we heard that the winner of Section 1 had also won the Saddler's Company Bridle for the best cross-country score for a competitor under 21. The winner of Section 1 patently wasn't under 21. I suddenly recalled a last minute change of rider. Didn't I inform the scorers? A frenzied call to Gina, who immediately, bless her, came back with the answer-Michael Heaton-Ellis. I might have known it! He particularly asked for very early times and had gone off to ride in a point to point! A rather elderly gentleman came to collect the prize in his place.

No rain until 3.30, when I was once again on the course watching the Advanced class.

Not so guilty this time, as Karen and Jan preferred to watch the Grand National, and Marilyn isn't interested in horses. Everyone was enthusiastic and full of thanks. Goodness knows how some of them managed their times. It was nearly over and we still had the terrier. Everything seemed to be running to time, and the Red Cross ambulances hadn't moved. Barry was at last relaxed and offering liquid sustenance to all and sundry. Daughter-in-law Jill offered to take the terrier home as she was worried about him. It might have been a solution but they already possessed a number of sheep, a dozen assorted hens, one pony, one cow, two calves, one pig, two cats, four dogs and a baby. The terrier didn't appear to be worried and was taken for his third walk.

Prize giving. Thanks from Tony Wootton, always graciously given, and an unexpected tribute from Mr. Boreham. Couldn't think why the Midland Bank should thank us. Sue Hatherly came second and gave Barry a sideways glance.

Suddenly it was all over and the place was almost empty, apart from the terrier. I suddenly remembered the Police, and dashed up a ladder where they had been chatting to Barry. 'They went off in a hurry' someone said. 'They were afraid you were going to ask them to take the terrier.' I was.

Why do we do it? I don't know. In retrospect it's fun. We make a lot of friends and we laugh a lot. We are also frequently exasperated and *always* worried.

Perhaps the answer is summed up best by an incident that took place the week after the trials. Having spent a lovely day at Downlands we drove back that first week of April, through a blinding storm of sleet and snow. At home our drive was flooded and as I opened the back door of the kitchen, there on the table lay a magnificent bouquet of carnations, tulips, and narcissi in glorious spring colours. Attached to it was a card that read simply 'From that Talland lot.'

Horses and Hunting

In 1975 we embarked on our horse rearing enterprise. Up to this time we had been producing in-calf heifers which were sold in Salisbury Market to dairy farmers. The milk trade was suffering one of its down turns in the early 70's so I decided to replace the heifer calves we had been buying with colt foals to be reared for Eventing. We were buying about 300 calves each autumn to be sold at two and a half to three years old so we had plenty of buildings, so I figured we could probably manage 100 colt foals each year to replace the heifers. The old adage - "Only fools buy foals" - is obviously correct as we finished up with six! And one of those was a home-bred out of a hunter mare! Anyway, it was a start and we decided to call them all names beginning with A. We followed this system all through and now have the last of the line - ZEUS. We shall not be starting again!

We eventually settled on buying 10 or 12 foals each year. Initially I put an advert in the Horse and Hound for "Good

Horses and Hunting

quality colt foals by T.B. or H.I.S. stallions" but after a year or so this became unnecessary as people came to know what we were doing and we were offered plenty.

Zeus – the last of the line

We spent many hours each autumn looking at foals and very interesting it was. We visited all sorts of places and in spite of the emphasis on potential eventers we saw everything from cart horses to ponies! Our final method of selection was first to see the dam, then look at the foal and if they both passed our (amateurish) scrutiny we would buy it. Strangely enough, although Jane knew very little about horses at the outset, she always had a good eye for a horse and it was often her opinion that carried the day. She was seldom wrong but even now she would be hard-pressed to explain why she liked (or disliked) a horse.

After a year or so trying to sell our youngsters at sales or privately we hit on the idea of holding bi-annual sales here at Rushall. These became something of a local social event, conducted by John Wallis as auctioneer, but we had to discontinue after 1991 when VAT at 17.5% was introduced as it priced our horses out of the market. The format we adopted was to parade all the horses for sale in the morning and to start the sale after lunch. We always had a bar in the barn to get people in a good mood and once we had a dressage demonstration on one of our horses by Angela Tucker in the lunch break. We offered the 2 y.o.'s, 3 y.o.'s and 4 y.o.'s for sale - the 4 y.o.'s being the 2 y.o.'s that had not sold in the previous sale - and we paraded the yearlings for people to see what we had in the pipeline. The horses were all held in yards at France Farm, Rushall and during the lunch break it was always pleasing to me to see people walking amongst them quite unperturbed by the general noise and bustle. We tried to produce well-mannered young horses for others to take on in whatever branch of riding that they wished.

The Yard on Sale Day

Initially we backed all the youngsters at two years old, but we found that most people preferred to do it themselves so we gave up! We backed 12 in one day - only one unauthorised dismount! - all done by Jimmy Hill's method. The one sadness to me was that very few eventers turned up at our sales, although this was the sport we were so keen to encourage. On reflection I realised that eventing riders do not have the facilities to keep youngsters for two or three years before they can compete them, but it would have been nice to see some of them on the ground that they rode over at the Horse Trials.

At our last sale in 1991 we included a page of "Old Boy" News. I wrote to everyone who had bought our horses and asked for an update on their progress. The most pleasing thing

Horses and Hunting

to me was to see how many remarked on their temperament as this was something that flowed from the way we were advised to treat them by Jimmy Hills and Harry Griffin. At Appendix C there is a copy of this "Old Boy" News. Incidentally, as this was to be our last sale we included the yearlings - including PLANTAGENET who didn't sell and who now has 668 B.E. points.

John Wallis selling

Chapter 10

SHOOTING CHANGES

As already recorded we enjoyed fabulous partridge shooting here in Wiltshire in the 1960's and 70's. At that time, in Wiltshire at any rate, farmers ran their own shoots, invited neighbouring farmer friends and used the men on the farm as beaters. On the larger places, a keeper was employed full time to control the vermin, chiefly rabbits and rats, and to protect as many nests as he could find. To a greater or lesser extent the Euston system was used to maximise the number of partridges hatched in natural nests. In the days when estates could employ many keepers the Euston system was devised which worked like this: every partridge nest would be found and the eggs replaced by dummies (wooden replicas). The trick was to ensure you collected the last egg from each nest so that nothing hatched until you replaced the dummies with "chipped" eggs. Should even one real egg be left in the nest the mother partridge would start "sitting" (incubating) and in due course the single egg would hatch and she would leave the nest with just one chick. So the egg collecting was an on-going exercise until the mother started sitting and she would continue sitting for as long as six weeks if the dummies were not replaced - the normal incubation period for a partridge is three weeks.

Shooting Changes

As the egg collecting proceeded the keeper would place them under bantams and in due course they would "chip". This meant that they had to be replaced in the nests on which the partridge was sitting on dummies. The eggs were not necessarily returned to their own nest - indeed it was beneficial to move eggs from one nest to another to effect a change of blood. The keeper would select those nests that were most vulnerable, either to vermin or human interference, to have the first clutches of "chipped" eggs so that they were at risk for a shorter time than the normal three weeks. Once replaced, the chipped eggs would hatch the next day provided the mother bird had not been frightened when the eggs were switched - an art in itself. The balance of the eggs would be distributed round the estate to the rest of the dummied nests.

The advantages of this system is that many more eggs would be hatched as all those nests destroyed during incubation would only lose dummy eggs - the real ones would be safely under bantams. The obvious drawback is that it is very labour intensive which is why it is not practised on a large scale today. Parker used a modified system where he only dummied vulnerable nests and distributed the chipped eggs to late or second nests that only had a small clutch, thus being left with very few partridge chicks to rear by hand with the help of the bantams.

Keepers, nowadays, are few and far between. The economics of shooting are such that where there were once five keepers there is now only one and where there was one there is now no-one or at best a part-time amateur. This means that true keepering is now very rare so vermin control is far less than once it was when we had tunnel traps in every hedge and fence line, in every wood or copse - in fact everywhere where vermin would run. One of my friends once said to me that if I started working out the costs of a day's shooting I would stop tomorrow! To overcome this problem there have been two significant developments. The first has been the virtual demise of the purely private shoot, which has been replaced by syndicates to spread the cost. There are two types of syndicate - one that takes a shoot and shoots it as often as they can afford and the other, the peripatetic syndicate that takes a day on one of the estates that lets days to help defray costs. Both have their advantages but both indicate how things have changed in the last forty years.

One of the most important things when organising a shoot, whether private or for a syndicate, is for the guests to feel that the runner of the shoot is really trying. Nothing is worse on a shoot than to have a good morning and then be restricted to outlying or poor drives because the required number of birds has already been shot. One memorable shoot to which I was invited as a guest is a case in point. My diary entry reads: "Quite the most remarkable day's shooting I've ever had! Suspected a light day when we had to put down our sweep numbers for the end of the day. I wanted to put 102 but our host said "No", so I said 62. Again "No". Then he said I could put 42. They had it on a blackboard and the scores varied between 6 and my 42! No numbers - first drive a small wood. (It was very wet and windy all day - no self respecting pheasant should have been above ground!) 5 beaters and 7 guns. Beaters very enthusiastic and remained so all day. We could hear them coming but no birds. Then suddenly all hell was let loose as a cock pheasant got up - to be missed by forward guns. That was drive No.1. The next

Shooting Changes

drive produced one hen pheasant and one pigeon. Also one fox that came along in front of me very sedately until he heard two shots which prompted him to leave covert. The next drive was a hedge and a few fields where 3 pheasants and 2 good coveys of partridges were seen but not hit. Then some game cover which consisted as far as I could see, of a thin hedge! Still blowing a gale and pouring with rain. One covey and one pheasant over the guns - nothing hit but the back gun shot a partridge which his dog promptly ate! Then to what we had been promised to be the best drive of the day - lunch! I was hopeful of a good warm fire in a pub with hot grub. But no - we sat or stood in a stone barn with no door on the gale end and had a picnic prepared by the ladies (4) who turned up just in time. Hot (?) soup and pie and salad, cheese, celery and coffee. Several hints were dropped that enough was enough but to no avail. So off we went, the gale making the rain seem like hail and it was impossible to face it. One pheasant was put up which sailed over the guns who didn't even see it! Another drive and some pigeon shooting ended the day. The bag: 1 Pheasant, 1 Partridge (eaten by dog) 4 Pigeons - Total 6., so I didn't win the sweep! A memorable day!" But how they all tried - host and beaters and guns.

This reminds me of a poem by Christopher Curtis sent to me by Robert Ferguson:

HI LOST!

Oh! The dogs in our shoot:
"Will you come here you brute"
You can hear them shout all down the line.
Untrained and unruly, I promise you truly
That the only exception is mine.

Shooting Changes

There's old Colonel Jack swearing flat on his back
With his gun pointing up in the air
You can hear how he felt, when attached to his belt
His young Labrador spotted a hare

Dick's bird hits the ground, four dogs make a bound
And arrive on the scene all together.
They divide it in three and, from what I can see
Dick's dog brings him back just one feather.

That spaniel of Joe's has a terrible nose
A fact that accounts for the reason
Why he mutters rude words as he looks for his birds
His dog hasn't found one all season.

Bob's not been too clever and used as a tether
His cartridge bag fixed to a stake
When a rabbit went past, his dog took off fast
With his bag, now they are both in the lake.

I cannot believe a worse Golden Retriever
Exists than the one owned by Jones
The only sound heard when he picks up a bird
Is the horrible crunching of bones.

But even that's better than Charles' Red Setter
Which is really the worst of the bunch
Having eaten a pheasant, it did something unpleasant
While we all sat around having lunch.

Shooting Changes

> *Like a bat out of hell and quite deaf to Jane's yell*
> *Goes her flat-coated dog being active*
> *In pursuit of a runner and, though Jane is a stunner*
> *Her dog I find far from attractive.*
>
> *No, you cannot dispute that the dogs on our shoot*
> *Are the worst ever seen in a line.*
> *Look, there goes one now and its chasing a cow*
> *Disgraceful! Good gracious, it's mine!*

Another important ingredient for a happy day's shooting is for the host to treat all the guns on a 'let' day as if they were his own friends. We did let several days at Rushall before I gave up shooting, and this didn't usually present a problem as the letter opposite from the Viscomte Bernard de la Giraudiere shows.

My game book records no "friends" in the sundries column so perhaps they were not very good shots!

However, you do occasionally find yourself hosting a group who only see shooting as a game of numbers and marksmanship. Of course, these people do not come again but if you are unlucky enough to have one such it can ruin the day for all concerned with the shoot. The worst case I came across was when, after a drive for pheasants one of the beaters, one of our farm men, pointed out to a gun where his bird had fallen. The gun said, "I came here to shoot, not to pick up".

The shoot at Rushall is now let to a syndicate of local people, several of whom live in the village. There are about 25 members and on shooting days half stand while the other half beats and vice versa. They put down a few birds and have great fun

Shooting Changes

```
                    CHAMPAGNE
              Vve Laurent-Perrier & Co.
                  ESTABLISHED 1812
```

Barry WOOKEY, Esq.
The Manor
UPAVON, PEWSEY
Wiltshire SN9 6EB
Grande-Bretagne

7th December, 1988

Dear Mr. Wookey,

    I thought I would just drop a note to tell you how much all our guests enjoyed the shoot we arranged on your estate last month.

    The birds flew very well - which could only have been helped by the excellent weather - and the drives arranged in a most excellent manner.

    Beyond this, I think that the terribly important factor is how nice you, your wife and the family are to the guests and how very much they feel like shooting at one of their friends'.

    Wishing you all a very Happy Christmas and new year,

Yours sincerely,

Vicomte Bernard de la Giraudière

during the season, although they would be the first to admit that they are not all good shots!

Chapter 11

ETNA AND SHIN

As already mentioned, I persuaded Bob Browning to come to Norway with me in 1991 when we had a completely blank week. Feeling somewhat guilty I took him for lunch at the Norge Hotel in Bergen on the way home. If you have never been to the Norge, don't miss the opportunity to visit it if ever you are in Bergen - it has some of the very best seafood you can possibly imagine! Anyway, Bob and I sat down to lunch and our waiter, a very slim Norwegian, soon started asking us if we were English and what were we doing in Norway. One thing led to another and it ended up with him giving us the telephone number of a friend of his who owned some salmon fishing on a river called the Etna which runs into the sea about half-way between Stavanger and Bergen. Like all fishermen he was full of enthusiasm and led us to believe that his friend's part of the Etna was paradise - lots of big fish only too eager to take our flies!

After a blank week on the Voss and after a few beers we thought we ought to give it a try. The coincidence of being waited on by someone who knew someone who had a wonderful river full of fish was too much for us so we decided to give this chap a ring when we arrived back home. After all, we reasoned, it couldn't be worse than the Voss and by all accounts it could be very much better! So I rang him and asked for details for next year (1992) and in due course he sent us a video showing his section of the Etna. All I remember of the video was that every cast seemed to hook a 20 lber. The river looked perfect fly water so we decided to give it a go in 1992.

We set out by car, plus our wives, Jane and Sheila, to catch the ferry from Newcastle to Bergen. It was an overnight crossing and I do remember the wonderful spread they put out on board for our supper. All the things I really like - prawns, salmon smoked and boiled, rare roast beef, crab, lobster - were there for us to help ourselves and I thought what a good way to start our holiday. I began filling my plate just as the boat reached the open sea and with every extra prawn I took I felt slightly more queasy. I soon had to give up the unequal struggle and escaped to our cabin where I spent a none-too-happy night!

After arriving at Bergen the next morning we motored down to the Etna. We seemed to use a dozen or so ferries over the many inlets on this Norwegian coastline and they were all spotlessly clean and they all ran bang on time. We reached Etna and were shown our chalet - very basic but passable. But we were there for the fishing and I have to report that we had a disappointing time, only managing two small salmon and a seatrout between us all week. My diary note says "Lovely place but short of two feet of water. A few fish in river". This brings to mind, then and on many occasions both before and after this visit, what an old Scottish ghillie once said to me "With salmon fishing, when everything's right, something's wrong." Bob and I hired a boat with an outboard motor one day to fish the estuary where a lot of salmon were said to be showing. We started off trolling and very soon I had a good pull and got very excited only to find it was a mackerel! Anyway, it gave us hope and we carried on until we noticed that the motor was gradually slowing down and eventually stopped. Somehow or other my line had fouled the propeller and was wound round and round enough to stall the engine. So we had to row to shore and spent about an hour untangling everything - rather an undignified way of salmon fishing! Needless to say we didn't catch a salmon.

On another day we took time off to go and see the locals at work on one of the other beats. This consisted of a fairly long run of fast water - almost a waterfall - which contained several pot-holes where the fish rested on their way up the falls. We didn't see one caught but their method was somewhat basic. They used a very long rod, a very strong line and dangled a bunch of worms into the pot-holes. We figured that if they hooked a fish they would have to swing it round to the bank as quickly as possible as there was no path they could use to follow it down to the pool below.

The only other thing I remember of this trip was bringing back our fish. The biggest was only 8 1/2 lbs. but was too long to go into our insulated fish carrier, so Bob decided we had to chop off its tail to get it in. It was deep-frozen by this time and we only had a bread saw-knife to cut it. Bob struggled and struggled and eventually we had a tail-less fish we could carry home. We again visited the Norge on the way back but "our" waiter was not in evidence - perhaps he had seen us coming!

The following year (1993) Jane and I again went to Etna. Neither of us can remember much about it and the total catch was nothing! Why we went we can't imagine but it was our last visit to Norway as most of the rivers have been closed to salmon fishing to try and conserve stocks. There was one highlight for me when I climbed a tree to watch two Norwegians take a 15 lb.

fresh fish on a fly. They often have ladders in trees so one can spot the fish while the other casts for it, and I was with the tree man and saw the salmon take. Very interesting. The flip side to this story is that as I was walking up to fish my beat which was just below theirs I came across them stoning my pool. When they saw me they moved on up to their beat and I believe they had seen a fish on my beat and tried to shift it onto theirs - with apparent success!

The Falls of Shin

After a pause to recover in 1994, 1995 saw the start of my trips to the Shin. This is one of four rivers that run into the Dornoch Firth, the others being the Carron, the Oykel and the Cassley. The Shin has the great advantage of a guaranteed

Minimum Flow, of even greater advantage in times of summer drought. I understand that when they dammed the river to create Loch Shin the riparian owners down-stream negotiated a deal whereby in times of low water the River Authority had to release sufficient water to maintain a predetermined flow. During our visits to the Shin we had reason to be very grateful to the previous owners because we always had water to fish even if there were no fish!

For many years before he sadly died, our friend Peter Scott became very keen on fishing and took a lot of the lower Wye and a beat on the Shin and invited his friends to share the fishing with him. I had many days on the Wye as his guest or as one of his rods over the years and I was invited to join his party on the Shin in 1995. This Peter Scott is not the one of Slimbridge renown, but our home-grown Wiltshire product who became the M.D. of T.H. White, Devizes and for a year was High Sheriff of Wiltshire. So I was delighted to join his party on the Shin and we had a really great time there with Jill Horton looking after us and the fish arriving on time - a vital requirement. Admiring the scenery palls after a few days if there are no fish to liven up proceedings! We always seemed to be lucky on the Shin as I see in my diary for the week 25 June - 1 July 1995, the Cassley and Oykel were "hopeless" and in 1998 I see I noted "Fish arrived as we did - previous week 1, before that 0". We had 22 that week.

Apart from the fishing which I thoroughly enjoyed, my diary reminds me of three interesting episodes. The first was in 1996. We were going down the steps to the Falls Pool, just below the Falls of Shin, a great tourist attraction, with the ghillie and we came to the locked gate which was meant to deter poachers. As the ghillie unlocked the gate he noticed a nice fresh salmon by the side of the path. He didn't seem surprised - he just said "Poachers" and told us to keep it! One way of making up the bag.

The second was in 1998. On the 1st July we were fishing away quite happily under a cloudless sky when the river started to rise very rapidly. According to my note it rose from 4 foot - 6 foot (depending on where you were on the river) in about an hour and subsided equally quickly. We later discovered that the rise had been due to a computer error at the main dam. Evidently a hazard of modern technology.

And the third episode was very personal. I was fishing the Falls Pool and was tackling up when I went to pick up my fly which had fallen to the ground. Unfortunately it was still attached to the cast on which I was standing with the result that the hook went into and through my left forefinger. The fly was a double hooked Ally Shrimp. Having nothing suitable to cut the hook above the barb I went up to the Tourist Centre above the Falls and asked the proprietor if he had any strong pliers to cut the hook. He tried with a big pair of scissors and some pliers to no avail except to make me wince a bit! This being no good I thought I had better visit the doctor in Bonar Bridge a few miles down the road. I had just got under way - the fly still sticking out of my finger- when I met three fishermen walking back to their car. I asked them if they had any sharp pliers but all they could produce was a pair of scissors, and I had had enough of scissors by this time. So on I went to Bonar Bridge and not knowing where the doctor lived I stopped and asked a lady tending some boxes of plants on the pavement if she knew if there was an ironmonger in town where I might find some strong pliers. "Yes", she said, "I am the ironmonger." So in I went to see what she had in the way of pliers. The first ones she showed me were ordinary ones and I thought not up to the job so she then produced a pair of real wire cutters - rather like overgrown nail clippers but very powerful. So I set to work on my finger and nipped off the free hook so that I could get out the one in my finger. While this was going on, with me operating on her counter, the lady ironmonger went a bit white. and disappeared! But the pliers did the trick - I still have them, with two nicks in the blades where they cut the two hooks - so I recalled the ironmonger and asked her if there was a local chemist where I could buy a dressing. No problem there so I was soon on my way with a plastered finger that rapidly recovered. The only snag was that I had told her I would buy the wire cutters if they did the job so after the "operation" I asked her the price - £38.50p. - which she very kindly said I need not pay - I think she was only too glad to get rid of me! However, conscience got the better of me and I went back and paid her the next day.

Chapter 12

GAME FAIR 26th,27th,28th July 1979

In the early summer of 1978 I had a 'phone call from Gerald Ward inviting me to the inaugural meeting of a committee he was forming to run the 1979 Game Fair at Bowood. He seemed to think that because we had run several Rushall Horse Trials by this time we would be qualified to run a section of the Game Fair! After a bit of thought, and in consultation with my wife and secretary, I agreed to attend the meeting thinking that I would be given the Fishing Section to organise as I knew nothing about Field Trialling or Clay Pigeon Shooting.

At the appointed date I presented myself at the meeting and listened to Gerald explaining how he had been appointed the local Chairman of the Game Fair under the overall supremo - Maj. Gen. Geoffrey Armitage, C.B.E. The whole Fair would be divided up into Sections, the main ones being Shooting, Fishing and Gun Dogs; each Section to be the responsibility of one person who would gather together a committee of knowledgeable experts. When all this had been explained he proceeded to announce the Section Chairmen, and you can imagine my surprise when he revealed that I had been given the Gun Dogs, about which I knew nothing in the competitive sense. I later - much later - learnt that he had appointed people to a Section that they were not familiar with so that they would start with a clean slate. My slate was very clean!

So I set about collecting a committee. I knew there would be experts to run the various competitions, so we were chiefly concerned with the admin. side of things. The first person I approached was Gordon Walch, a retired Brigadier, who had helped us with our Horse Trials from the very beginning. He was one of those people who could always be relied on to get everything he undertook done properly and he was also very tactful, so I put him in charge of people. He was also one of those men who could deliver a rocket with a smile on his face but the recipient was left in no doubt that he had done something not quite right. He dealt with everyone connected with the Gun Dogs - the Judges, the Demonstrators, the participants, the stewards and all the rest of the volunteers who helped us on the three days.

Next we needed someone to be in charge of things - the tables and chairs, the food, the prizes and anything that went wrong on the day, so I invited Peter Lemon to do this and thankfully he accepted and did the job very well. As in all one-off events there are always a few crises to sort out and as my brother-in-law, Thomas Flynn, said in a letter he wrote to me afterwards, Peter dealt with all these "with speed and good humour."

And we had to have a Secretary and once again our farm secretary, Marilyn Treverrow, agreed to do this. I say "once again" as she not only looked after the secretarial side of two large farms, she also helped us with everything we undertook - the Horse Trials, the Triathlon, my Court work, Jane's Council work and my books. She has now been with us for 33 years and we are not the only ones who appreciate all her hard work as another letter, this time from Wilson Stephens after the Game Fair reflects - "May I ask you to pass my thanks and admiration also to the superb Marilyn."

"Ashton's Eerie" and some of the crowd

Next we needed an "anchor man" in the commentary box we had persuaded Maj. Gen. Armitage to provide for the Gun Dog Section. We already had an in-house commentator for the Horse Trials so I asked Charles Ashton if he would do it. I assured him that he would have someone with him as the technical expert on the various competitions, but what we needed was someone who could keep the show alive between the stints by the experts. I felt he was well qualified to do this as a letter I had after one of our first Horse Trials from his ex-commanding officer shows. "The real touch of genius was to put Charles Ashton on the microphone. As his commanding officer, I spent a couple of years trying to stop him talking. You accepted his talent and channelled it into useful work." He, too, made a great success of Ashton's Eerie with Wilson Stephens and Peter Flecchia to keep him in order!

To complete the admin. part of the committee we invited John Wallis, the agent for Bowood to join us. As he lives near us and is also our agent for Rushall it all came together very well. Jane also helped when she could, especially with the V.I.P.'s. The experts from the Dog World were:

J.W. Davey and R.H. Hill	International and Mixed Doubles
P.J. Taylor and G. Thompson	Pick-up and Scurry
R. Davis and G. Cox	Information Centre and Training Demonstrations
D.M. Layton	Sporting Dogs

The main competition was the International Match consisting of two sets of Tests, one for Retrievers and one for Spaniels, for teams of dogs from the four home countries. Each country produced a team of four retrievers and four spaniels. Messrs. Davey and Hill ran this with no input from us except to ensure that the teams arrived on time. The traffic into Bowood was tremendous and the Irish, who insisted on staying in Bristol, were our chief worry. They always seemed to have a party the night before so getting to the ground each morning in time proved a problem! The Mixed Doubles, a new competition this year, turned out to be a great success. It was run on the Thursday only by our two stalwarts, Messrs. Davey and Thompson and was sponsored by Peter Dominic whose Press Officer, Janet Browne, wrote to me afterwards - "I felt the Mixed Doubles went extremely well and we certainly got lots of lovely mentions for Dominic - sorry if I nagged you so much!" She was certainly very assiduous in her job - I firmly believe she sat under a loud-speaker all day with a watch and if more than ten minutes went by without Charles Ashton saying something nice about Dominic she would chase after me and demand why!

The competition consisted of a series of tests for one handler with two dogs, one a recognised hunting and retrieving breed and the other a recognised retrieving breed. It was a bit complicated to remember all the tests but, as this extract from an article in the Shooting Times and Country Magazine of 9 August 1979 shows, the pessimists were proved wrong:

"I frequently find myself having to eat my words, and this I most certainly must do after my pessimistic forecast about the Mixed Doubles event (sponsored by Peter Dominic) at the Game Fair! Especially considering the heat and the obvious lack of scent on the very light soil, the great majority of dogs went extremely well, both on land and in water, and handlers did not get into too many difficulties .... The obvious success of this event leads me to hope and believe that it will become an established feature of the Game Fair."

This was the first Game Fair to be run over three days (previously only two) and this, coupled with the fact that there was a real heat-wave over the whole time, could have frayed a few tempers but I can honestly say that the team we had was excellent and I don't think anyone from the public detected any of our little problems. We were also honoured with a visit from Prince Charles who was particularly interested in the Pick-up and Scurry which were open to anyone with a suitable dog. He seemed to have wished he had brought one of his own, but as he hadn't he spent some time watching the competitors who varied in skill from 0 to 10! The Pick-up consisted of six dummies hidden in the allotted area. The dogs had to collect as many as possible as fast as possible within a maximum of three minutes. The Scurry required each dog to retrieve two thrown dummies, one from water and the other from ground cover, in as fast a time as possible. Both these competitions were very well supported by the visiting public and were both sponsored by Nicholson Sloe Gin, who very kindly presented us with a case. When thanking them I said that as it was so hot we would keep it until we were shooting in the winter as I always thought of Sloe Gin as a winter drink. However, Richard Nicholson, the Managing Director at the time, soon put me right by saying it was the ideal drink for hot weather - when taken with ice and tonic. He was right and I think we, the staff, sank most of it over the three days of the Game Fair! We found it so good that we drink all the bottles I make every year in this way leaving none for the shooting season!

The Bristol and West Working Gundog Society (B.W.W.G.S.) in the shape of Roger Davis and Graham Cox, were invaluable. They provided many of their members to help with the stewarding etc. as well as running the Gundog Training Demonstrations and the Advice Centre. They also persuaded me to hold a Field Trial on our farm later in the year. Field Trials are something of a closed book to me and I'm afraid we didn't do a very good job. My note in my Game Book reads: "Almost a disaster. Harrier ruined partridges so went on to pheasants. Marvellous lunch." (provided by B.W.W.G.S.) Graham Cox who attended and who wrote an account of the day in their magazine, was rather more tactful! He wrote - "Having served on the Game Fair Gundog Committee earlier in the year under the excellent chairmanship of Barry Wookey, both Roger Davis and I were delighted that B.W.W.G.S. was able to hold a trial on his rolling Wiltshire downland. We knew that exacting standards of efficiency and organisation would be set by our host and his Head Keeper Mr. Fred Dark." The main purpose of the day was to provide partridges for the contestants and we had invited the Director of the Game Fair, Maj. Gen. Geoffrey Armitage C.B.E. as one of the guns. Graham's report goes on "The carefully contrived silence was only punctuated by the occasional distant boom from artillery fire as Fred Dark and his line of beaters appeared on the horizon during the first drive, but surprisingly no partridge appeared and this experience was repeated on the second drive." Not a very auspicious start! We went on to pheasants and found just enough for the judges to produce a winners list. Graham's account ends "So, although there was only one partridge retrieve all day the Trial was an exacting one and handlers were grateful for the patience and care which the judges showed during a long and demanding day. They were warmly thanked for their efforts, as was our host for making such an absorbing day possible." He should have been a diplomat! I feel it was a poor return for all their kindness, hard work and enthusiasm that they extended to us at the Game Fair but we did try!

Game Fair

We found the whole Game Fair great fun and very exhausting in the heat. We met lots of people and all were very kind and appreciative. Because I had thought I would have been asked to undertake the Fishing Section, I wandered over there one day and tried my hand at the casting competition. As I had done a lot of practising for the Triathlon I thought I could hit a few targets and a few days later I received a £10 prize with a note from the Director! I stuck it in my scrap book with the comment "To prove I should have been given the Fishing."

And to round off the experience, we were sent a very fine Christmas Card from the Rushall and District Clay Pigeon Club who use our old chalk pit for shooting and who also helped in July, with a photograph of two spaniels and a labrador on the front taken at the Bowood 1979 Game Fair.

Game Fair

Gundogs at Bowood

Chapter 13

GERRY'S PIKE

This is the account of another pike caught by Gerry Quincy (who now looks after the Rushall fishing) and his friend and fellow rod, Bob Simmons. The date was 31st July 2003 and the two streams are the eastern and western branches of the Upper Avon where they meet just below Scales Bridge, between Upavon and North Newnton.

About 40 or 50 yards below where the two streams meet there is a pool adjacent to the new rod rest. I was fishing the pool with a nymph and hooked a brown trout of approximately 10 inches at the far end of the pool. The bank is steep and I moved upstream in order to use the landing net, whilst holding the trout at the top of the pool. I was looking down trying to find a foothold and heard a loud splash and felt a pull on the rod. It was obviously a pike but I didn't see it. When I reeled in all that was left was the lip of the fish!

Next day (not my fishing day but I believe justified on this occasion) I fished a 6 inch silver minnow through the pool. My initial assumption was that the pike's lie was under the near bank, in an eddy, which has cover, but there was no interest. Nor was there any interest in the middle of the pool. Finally I fished the far side by floating down and pulling across the pool. Almost immediately a pike followed the plug in and again on the next cast. On the third cast it made a halfhearted pass but thereafter lost interest. My estimate of the weight was 6 to 9 lbs. I tried a different plug and spoon but to no effect. (In retrospect I was probably lucky not to have connected; the gear was a very light trout rod, not much more than 6 or 7lb breaking strain and no gaff plus a steep bank). Reinforcements were needed so I rang Bob Simmons and we decided to have a go for it next day.

Bob Simmons writes:

I had been pike fishing only twice before, without success, and never bothered to get the proper tackle. All I have in the way of spinning tackle is a spindly little rod and a tiny reel which I had given to my son when he was 10, and with which he proudly caught a very small bleak in the Thames. Under Gerry's tutelage I tried to catch pike on the Rushall Fishing with this rod a couple of years ago, but it was never tested, and when Gerry suggested that I should have a go at his evidently large pike, I felt a certain amount of apprehension about the tackle. I also possess, but have never used, some gadgets for dead baiting which look as if they are out of the torture chamber, and a sort of stuffed fish with some hooks dangling out of it. These had belonged to my father-in-law and I think to his father before him. Then I have a box with assorted spoons and Mepps, which I had bought years ago for sea trout fishing in Devon and a few pike flies someone gave me.

In the end it seemed that casting just a short distance with a spinning rod would be awkward and one would be better off with a fly rod, especially if the flies were to be used. So I chose a

Gerry's Pike

10 foot #8 trout rod and a floating line. I found a wire trace and a few rather flimsy swivels and some 20 lb nylon, and tied them together.

In the morning Gerry and I arrived at the scene of the crime and he told me what he had tried the day before. I put on one of my pike flies and tried to cast it where he indicated. The idea was to drop the fly at the top of a deep run where Gerry thought the pike was lying. This was only a couple of rod lengths downstream but it was close to the far bank and across the main flow. So to get the fly to sink and drift down the lie, some line had to be released quickly before the main stream caught the belly of the fly line and swept the fly out of the lie. I succeeded a couple of times, but nothing happened. Then we remembered that Barry had caught a couple of pike on a spotted Mepps, and put one of these on. As soon as I managed a decent cast and the line straightened in midstream, a green shape shot across the pool towards the Mepps, but it didn't take. The same thing happened again on the next cast, then nothing. I tried Gerry's plug, a spoon and the stuffed fish, but no response.

It seemed likely that by now we had put the pike down or chased it away. We looked hard to see if we could see it, but we couldn't. The water was crystal clear, but the flow was a bit turbulent so we couldn't see clearly to the bottom, and at any rate the pike would have been camouflaged in the weed. So we decided to go down to Upavon where I had caught a large number of grayling two days before, and if successful this time, to use the grayling as deadbait. Actually we did very well. In spite of the unwelcome attentions of an inquisitive horse which tried to eat Gerry's net, we got about 10 trout between us - nearly all of them Game Conservancy Trust tagged fish (all returned), and

5 grayling, and after a fortifying lunch at the Antelope we returned to the pike in a confident mood.

Gerry insisted that I have a go at dead baiting, and I hooked a grayling on to the least complicated of the contraptions. It was quite a weight, and it was hard to lob it on to the right spot - most of the time the bait hit the main flow in the middle of the river, or I didn't let out enough line and the bait was pulled away into the main stream too soon. Finally I managed to hit the target zone and let slip some slack line, and the bait was carried downstream for a yard or two near the far bank, then was pulled by the current across into midstream. This time a green shape circled round downstream of the bait and closed in on it. The bait disappeared and the line stopped. I tightened. "Have you got it?" called out Gerry, and I had.

The pike immediately went down to the bottom of the pool, and it felt very solid. Then I remembered seeing a film of someone catching a pike, and all that happened was it stayed down for a long time, and then finally was yanked up snapping and thrashing around on the surface, it was gaffed, and that was it. The only snags about this method for us were that my tackle was untrustworthy, so winding in a large struggling fish was not to be contemplated, and all we had was a trout net.

While the pike was boring down we surveyed the geography and it was unpromising. The pool itself had a few nasty hazards, with dense patches of weed on the bottom and reeds on the far bank. But the worst thing was the bank on our side which was both steep and high - very difficult to net a large fish from it. Below our pool the river widened out in long straight shallows, also with a steep high bank, though at the tail end it was possible to get down to the river. But getting there wasn't going to be easy; on the way there were a couple of trees close to the bank with roots in the river, and these could turn out to be a real obstacle. However, for the moment we had to tire the pike out, and just in case it was possible to net it, Gerry stationed himself at the tail end of the pool, though he could only just about touch the water with the end of his trout net.

I kept a fair amount of pressure on the pike, as much as I dared, and after five or ten minutes it came up. It swam around towards the tail of the pool, still deep in the water and after a while I was able to pull it up a bit and steer it towards Gerry and the net. But when it saw the net, it exploded, surging across the surface of the river and crashing into the reeds on the other bank. Fortunately the line didn't snag, but we realised the fish had to be treated with respect. This kind of activity was repeated a number of times, including a long surge downstream out of the pool, when my heart was in my mouth because of a tree root at the tail of the pool just beyond Gerry. I managed to drag the pike back, but finally it made a dive for the tree root and seemed to be tangled and I had to run along the bank to the tree, but luckily the line freed itself. By this time we had seen the pike on the surface and realised it was big, and that landing it was a serious problem.

Now that the fish was at the top end of the shallows, Gerry suggested letting it swim further downstream to the spot some 50 yards lower down where he could get down the bank to net it. First though we had to get round the trees. I handed the rod to Gerry round the first tree and he gave it back to me and I got back in contact with the pike again. It was now on the surface, but still not really under control, surging across the river each time I tried to bring it over to our bank. But I led it downstream, and successfully negotiated the rod round the next tree. The pike swam down towards Gerry, now poised down the bank at the tail end of the shallow stretch, but then it darted across to the other bank. At this point I realised there was a fatal flaw to our plan, that if the pike decided to head off further downstream, we would run out of bank and undoubtedly be in serious difficulties.

Gerry's pike with Bob Simmons

Gerry's Pike

Luckily I was able to pull it upstream and then across to our bank, and I let it lead me at walking pace downstream towards Gerry and the waiting net. It swam straight towards them, and Gerry netted it very professionally - not an easy task with a small net. I put the rod down and slid down the bank and grabbed the net and we dragged the whole thing up the bank. Gerry knocked the pike on the head, and it was all over.

We shook hands and repaired to the caravan for a stiff whisky. With a mixture of weights and bricks we managed to weigh the pike - 13lb 14oz.

Though I held the rod, I will always think of it as "Gerry's Pike".

Chapter 14

PLANTAGENET   (by Jane)

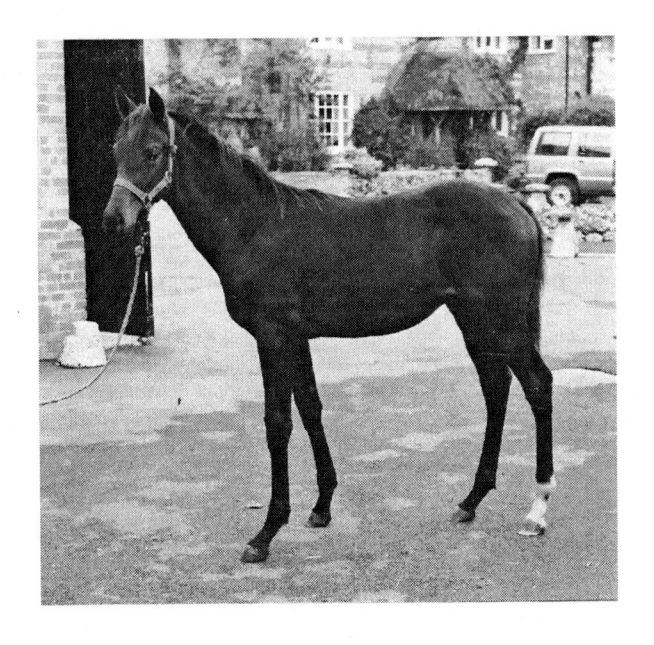

As a foal - 1990

Over the last 30 years we must have had a vast number of horses through our hands, mostly good, a few disappointing. Inevitably there were favourites among those we kept, but there

Plantagenet

is one who, at least to me, was in a class of his own and who, happily, is still with us. I know Barry would agree, although he is loath to admit it, possibly because I am biased enough for both of us!

We bought the foal in the autumn of 1990 on our way back from Blenheim. The lady who bred him was insistent that she delivered him to us, accompanied by his mother to ease the trauma. However in the end she was obliged to ring us to ask for help as she couldn't load them into her box!

We called him Plantagenet and in course of time Barry added "of Rushall" to the horse's name. This has become a custom when any of our horses start to compete seriously. I have always thought it rather pretentious, but it was a good advertisement when we were in the business of selling horses, and it means that our friends and neighbours recognise that the horses are local.

Plantagenet was a character from the very first. He is a dark brown thoroughbred and I think very beautiful, with a strikingly handsome head and a kind eye. He loves life and still, at the advanced age of 16, will squeal and buck through sheer excitement. His sire was a hurdler, Ra Nova, and strangely enough, Mark Perrett, the nephew of Badger, our horse expert on the farm, had raced Ra Nova a number of times.

When Plantagenet was four we asked Angela Tucker, who has been a friend for as long as I can remember and who is an immaculate rider with a special talent with young horses, to take him on and introduce him to the Burghley Young Event Horse competition. This is an excellent "starter" for young horses hoping to go on to event, and helps them to become familiar with crowds, noise and general activity. Unfortunately, Angela developed a bad back so she suggested a young Swedish pupil of hers, Dag Albert, to take her place. Dag eventually qualified Plantagenet at Gatcombe for the Burghley finals but they finished about halfway down the list.

The following season the horse won his second Pre-Novice event and then started at Novice level. At the end of the year he had amassed four points! His jumping was invariably outstanding, but he was far too excitable in the dressage arena and found it all a big bore, particularly as he knew perfectly well what was to follow. Dag finally suggested that we entered the horse in Intermediate classes, which fazed him not at all, and he won at Longleat on his third attempt at that level. There were a number of other successes but as the competition became more demanding, it was clear that dressage was Plantagenet's weakness.

Angela Tucker winning at Burgie

Plantagenet

Dag had a lot of horses at the time and not much help, so we did the obvious and asked Angela, the dressage queen, to take the horse in hand. I well recall a trip to Chepstow when the horse refused to stand still in the Dressage arena. Angela's punishment was to withdraw him after showjumping and deny him his fun across country!

The combination was extremely successful, culminating in a win at Burgie Two Star, in the most appallingly wet conditions. The pair achieved much success, but Angela had always said that there would come a time when she felt that she had done enough, and that Plantagenet would benefit from a younger rider. So in 1999, and on Angela's recommendation, the horse was moved to the yard of Graham Law near Burford. We were anxious that he would remain reasonably close to home so that we could follow his fortunes.

Graham was an extremely competent and determined rider. After a few early setbacks, when Plantagenent displayed a certain reluctance at some water jumps, which we had noticed once or twice earlier, the pair had a remarkable run of 22 One Day outings, when they came lower than 10th only once, and that at Tweseldown, always a difficult event to finish in the money as it is so popular and so accessible and many people jump the cross-country clear. Most of these outings with Graham were at Advanced level, and they won twice - at Hartpury and Brockenhurst.

The first really big challenge was Blenheim 3 Star in the autumn of 1999. The dressage was awful and horse finished that phase in 65th place out of a huge class of over 90. However the next day he flew round the cross-country and came home half a minute inside the time. He was, at the end, extremely distressed and, for the first time, we wondered whether Graham's large frame was going to prove too much for the horse at a three day event. On the Sunday they show jumped clear and completed in 11th place, much to our delight.

Punchestown followed in the spring of 2000 when again the pair finished 11th. The dressage was better this time, although a heavy storm of driving rain greeted their entry into the dressage arena, and the judges were faced with Plantagenet's rear! The cross-country produced no problems for us but unfortunately one or two of the senior riders had complained about the time limit, so the Ground Jury added another 30 seconds. Thus quite a few horses finished within the time and Plantagenet's incredible speed, which has brought him up the order on so many occasions over the years, was of no great advantage this time.

Burghley in September and our first 4 Star. A dressage of 59.6 at this level was quite a relief, and two time faults on the cross-country was the fastest of the day. That evening we were lying in 4th place and I remember thinking that we were unlikely to be in as high a position as that at a 4 Star ever again. It was the year when the powers that be were experimenting with a different scoring system, and each second over the time limit on the cross-country invoked one penalty point. Great for Plantagenet! Sadly nerves seemed to take over both horse and rider on show jumping day, normally not a problem, and they had the first fence down. Graham was meticulously careful after that but they incurred seven time faults and dropped to 10th place. Under other circumstances we would have been thrilled at the outcome, but the inevitable reaction was "so near and yet so far."

Plantagenet

As a 3 year old with Claire Latham

Burghley the following year was rather a disaster as the horse produced a splint. The dressage judges marked him right down as they considered him unsound and he was withdrawn. This was his last outing with Graham as we had to face the fact that, if we wished the horse to continue competing at top level, we needed a lighter jockey.

Jeanette Brakewell next stop, again on Angela's advice. At the time she lived in Norfolk, a nightmare of a journey for us, so we missed several of her earlier outings with him. Their first success was a 2nd in an Advanced Section at Belton and then she took him on to his first Badminton, which would have been a triumph except that the horse jumped the wrong side of the flag at the

Vicarage V, was charged a stop and had to go back and retake the fence. Twenty seven time faults were added to the stop so, despite a clear show jumping, he finished in 41st place. None-the-less Jeanette was satisfied!

Burghley that year was our high point. He finished 9th on a score of 63.41, the only horse to complete on his dressage score, and we were enormously proud. Jeanette was also 8th on the lovely grey, The Busker, so she had a wonderful weekend.

At Badminton in 2003 Plantagenet produced his best ever dressage test with a score of 50.8 and we were thrilled. Cross-country day was miserable with continuous drizzle and heavy going. Our pair were near the end of the day and I have never felt more apprehensive. It must have been noticeable, as I passed Angela outside the Supporter's tent and she said "Don't worry, he's a class horse and she's a class jockey." They came home safely with just 1.6 time faults. Jeanette had been worried about him that week as unusually he had been off his food, but he must have forgotten that on the Saturday. On Sunday they came into the show jumping arena in 8th position and we were full of optimism. One fence had already caused particular problems - a water jump with a vivid blue base immediately beside the Members' enclosure. The sun was shining on the water and reflecting the poles, and the breeze was causing ripples. As the horses came round the edge of the arena to face the fence many were startled and knocked it. The next fence was a related distance, so that proved a problem too. Jeanette decided to take Plantagenet inside the normal route, so that he didn't see the fence until the last minute. When he did he was so taken aback that he stopped dead and knocked it down. She retook the fence which he cat jumped and consequently hit the

Plantagenet

next. This disaster cost him 27 faults, including time faults, and although he sailed over the next seven fences, he dropped down to 25th place.

Burghley 2003 marked his last 4 Star outing. He was going well until he knocked himself going into the Trout Hatchery, and stopped coming back into the adjacent fence. I think he felt discretion was the better part of valour, so Jeanette withdrew. him. It was a very sad day. As always we had been full of hope and even expectation, but the horse didn't owe us anything. He had given us an immense amount of pride and enjoyment over a long period of time, added to which he had had the questionable distinction of being on the long list for the British Team for four successive years!

After that we knew we couldn't ask Jeanette to continue with him, as there was a chance that he might let her down again. She suggested trying a young rider, as the horse clearly didn't consider himself "over the top" and he enjoyed the sport so much that we felt he was not ready to retire. We consulted our favourite horse mentor yet again, and she knew of a friend and neighbour who would fill the bill.

So Plantagenet spent his 14th year in the company of 19 year old Louisa Brassey. She had her disappointments with him, chiefly when he was spun, to most people's amazement, while lying 6th after the cross-country in a huge class at Windsor. But she produced some lovely dressage tests and no longer does my heart stand still when he enters the arena. She ended the season with a win at Gatcombe in a class of 98.

Sadly, the Spring of 2005 was not so successful. He went very well at Aston-le-Walls but looked lack-lustre at Aldon and inexplicably stopped three times at the first Show Jump at

Plantagenet

Gatcombe, which was completely out or character. So the Brasseys decided to part with him.

Thus Plantagenet moved yet again, this time to another young rider, Lucie McNichol, who lives twelve miles from us and already had a 10-year-old of ours, Upmarket. Plantagenet has had a very happy year, revelling in the attention he has received and thoroughly enjoying competing at Intermediate level. He looks extremely well and still bucks and squeals with excitement. One day he will retire but he certainly isn't ready for that yet.

Flying at Badminton

Chapter 15

ODDS AND ENDS

When I started researching for this book, I went through all my old records and jotted down any incident that I thought might interest the reader. As the period stretches from 1948 to 2005 you can imagine that there are many items, only a very few of which have been covered in preceding chapters. So I went through all the items I had selected and reduced them as ruthlessly as I could. Every incident noted brings back very vividly the actual event so I have selected a sample to include in this chapter. They are in no particular order, they do not all refer to Field Sports but they all made an impression on me that I can still recall after 30, 40 or 50 years.

On our shooting days over the years we always had two, sometimes three, forms of entertainment. We had a sweep on the bag, as most shoots do, we had the half crown game and we sometimes, when there were plenty of young (and young in heart) present, had a rather raucous game of "table tennis". The sweep is well-known, the half crown game (what would we use now, I wonder - 50p?) was a simple gamble at tea-time after the shoot. Everyone had to start with three coins, everyone placed one on the table and the minority of heads or tails was out. The remainder repeated the process until two people were left and they tossed three times to decide the winner. We always had three rounds only so you stood to lose a maximum of seven and sixpence, or a good deal more if all the family were playing!

The "table tennis" was the greatest fun and usually ended up with everyone cheating! We had an old dining room table where we had tea, about ten feet long and three wide. To play this game the room had to be cleared of anything breakable. The company was divided into teams of two, each team being provided with a tennis ball and they had to start by one member of each team standing at each end of the table. The scoring was as for tennis. The referee had a half crown coin and to start the game he placed this in the centre of the table. The object of the game was to hit the coin from the table by throwing the tennis ball and the team that did it scored a point. By the end of the evening you were lucky if anything in the room survived!

On the 7th of January 1970 I was shooting with a friend and I see from my diary that there were "6 20-bores out - becoming fashionable!" I myself started with the usual .410 and progressed to a 20 bore - a lovely little gun. I then promoted myself to a 12 bore until the day I decided it was too easy - you should never miss a pheasant with a 12 bore! - and reverted to my original 20 bore. This was a Leeson double barrel double choke and with it I managed to miss many pheasants! The advantages of a 20 bore are many - it is lighter and therefore easier to mount, you can carry many more cartridges in your pockets and it will kill anything if you point it straight! So to have six out on the same day was quite remarkable.

"Filling the line" is something I have often tried but never succeeded. My game book has nine columns which are Pheasants, Partridges, Woodcock, Snipe, Mallard, Teal, Pigeons, Hares and Rabbits. My ambition was to shoot at least one of all

Odds and Ends

these on the same day by myself but, as I say, it proved too difficult. I walked miles when I was young and fit trying for it but the best I can see I recorded was 3/9! Incidentally, we never achieved it on any of our formal shooting days although we weren't specifically trying to do it then.

On the 9th of February 1970 I had a day with the Heythrop. Charles Ashton, whose friend was Hunt Secretary, came with me. In those far off days the Hunt Secretary received £600/year and in the last year they had spent £4000 on opening up their country - jumps, gates, bridges and taking down wire. The cap was £5! My diary reads "Had a good day. Enjoyed watching Ronnie Wallace hunting hounds. First fox a ringer and they killed him on the fourth circuit. Then a nice hunt with a lot of jumping. To ground. Plenty of foxes."

Testwood - 11 May 1970. Had day to myself (with Jack Terry, the ghillie) and had two, 10 ½ and 11 lbs. I had bought a Telegraph on the way down to show Jack our son Nigel's 105 not out for Malvern v The Gentlemen of Worcestershire, but it was a different edition and wasn't in it!

In June 1970 we suffered the first of our three cases of pollution. All were caused by thunderstorms bursting the banks of slurry lagoons on dairy farms upstream of our water and all were devastating. In this particular incident, I happened to be on the river when I noticed fish coming to the surface and seeming to gasp for breath. Not having seen this before it took me a little time to realise what was happening. The smell of dung became apparent and as the fish started dying I reported it to the River Authority who sent an inspector to check. Meantime, we tried to net the trout and resuscitate them in clean water but to no avail, only saving five. We collected the dead fish and buried one hundredweight of coarse fish and the same of brown trout, the best being 2 1/2 lbs. with many of 1 lb., good fish for our small river. The real sadness of this pollution is that it occurred on a stretch of river that was purely wild as we had never stocked it. It contained beautiful wild brown trout whose flesh was as pink as any salmon. Although the river was re-stocked by the culprit's insurers, it will probably never be the same again.

Another case of pollution was prosecuted by the River Authority and the case came up on a day I was sitting on the Bench. I arranged for it to be heard in the second court so that it wouldn't come up before me. As so often happens in court proceedings, the timing can be very imprecise. In this instance, the court due to take the case was held up by something or other and so the Clerk asked me to take it. When I said I was involved he told me that it was quite all right for me to hear it as the defendant had already pleaded guilty and it was only a matter of sentence. Somewhat reluctantly I allowed myself to be persuaded to take it and so was faced by John Wallis, agent for the offender and our own agent and who now has a rod on our water at Rushall, making a passionate plea in mitigation! This incident occurred when the maximum fine was, I think, £200. Very shortly afterwards, the maximum fine was increased to £2000. I didn't hesitate in telling John how lucky his client was!

Of all the visitors we have had over the years the most distinguished was, without doubt, H.R.H. The Prince of Wales, who came to look round our organic farm on 5 November 1984. He showed a great interest in what we were doing and subsequently adopted the system himself. A rather amusing incident occurred on the morning of his visit, before he actually arrived. The police were making a routine search of the premises

Odds and Ends

when my wife had occasion to call our son's dog. This black labrador was with Stephen in London before he moved to Paris, but because of import regulations he felt he couldn't take the dog, who was left with us. He was not always the most obedient of animals and often had to be called several times and in rather a loud voice. His given name was Charles Le Chien, but, as can be imagined, this was almost invariably reduced to "Charlie". So when, on the morning of the royal visit, my wife started calling "Charlie, Charlie", one of the detectives came up to her and said quietly, "Madam, today I think we will call him Rex."

Diary extract. 14 February 1973. "On holiday in Kenya. Deep sea fishing off Mombasa. Started 7 a.m. Four rods rigged trolling herring sized fish. Began just off the reef and went parallel to it. Evidently the big fish come to the reef at night and go out to sea by day. After about one and a half hours a marlin took one of the baits. Pandemonium! The skipper grabbed the rod and struck, held on while the fish went about 300 yards then struck three times again and gave me the rod in the chair. I never saw the fish but the skipper said it was a big marlin. They kept the boat going all the time and it was a case of pumping to get line back. Fish went very sullen and deep and I couldn't move it. It came up a bit and then sank to the bottom again. Hard work - shade temperature 96 degrees. A lady guest aboard was ill and violently sea-sick! After about one and half hours (possibly more) while I was pumping away the line fouled one of the rings, frayed and parted. So ended the fight in favour of the marlin. The boatman estimated it as 200 lbs. and Toby (a fellow guest on board) said its head looked as big as the record in the Club House - 409 lbs.!" Of the four rods out, the fish selected the oldest and tattiest one for his breakfast - the others were all spanking new!

One day in the 1970's I recall very vividly. I happened to be in the mill one morning when a customer walked in - quite an event in the early days. The man running our mill then was an ex-soldier called Sid Bird - "Dickie", naturally, to the others on the farm - and we started talking to the visitor, who turned out to be an employee of one of the milling giants in the country. He bought a 25 kg. bag and Sid and I felt we had done a good morning's work, selling a bag of flour to a representative of such a large miller.

About three weeks later I was in the mill again when in walked the same man. This time he was carrying our bag of flour, by now half empty, and we could see at once that he was far from happy. He put his hand into the bag and pulled out a very dead mouse. He sounded off quite well for a few minutes, saying how disgraceful it was to see a bag of flour with a dead mouse in it, and how upset his wife had been to find the mouse in the bag. I was struck completely dumb - I didn't know what to say or do, but I remember thinking how delighted this man's firm would be to take us to court and that it would probably be the end of our business. Not so Sid! With all his years of experience in the sergeant's mess coming to his aid, he took the dead mouse, examined it minutely and then handed it back with the words, "It's not one of ours, sir."

Jimmy Hills, former Brigadier, has already been mentioned in connection with horses. He was also a very keen fisherman, of the old school, fly only! He owned a vintage Rolls - yellow and black - of which he was very proud. Whenever he came fishing with us he would arrive in the Rolls and I always asked him to

Odds and Ends

park it in the centre of our drive in full view from the road - to improve our image! He also owned and drove an old Morris (247,000 miles on the clock) and on the way down to Testwood one day we were talking about speeding and limits when Jimmy said "I was cautioned for speeding the other day in my old Morris. The policeman said I was doing 38 m.p.h. I was delighted!"

I came across the following series of definitions on my travels and I reproduce them here as they always raise a smile when I read them again.

"COMMUNISM: You have two cows. The government takes both of them and gives you part of the milk.

"SOCIALISM: You have two cows. The government takes one and gives it to your neighbour.

"FACISM: You have two cows. The government takes both of them and sells you the milk.

"NAZISM: You have two cows. The government takes both of them and shoots you.

"BUREAUCRACY: You have two cows. The government takes both of them, shoots one and milks the other, then pours the milk down the drain.

"CAPITALISM: You have two cows. You sell one of them and buy a bull".

Odds and Ends

Other notes I made in a special book kept for the purpose appear as an Appendix. They cover the period from 1943 to 1957 and perhaps reflect how my sense of humour has developed! The final one, included here, seems a good place to end these memoirs.

The curfew tolls the knell of parting day
The line of cars winds slowly o'er the lea
The pedestrian homeward plods his absent-minded way
And leaves this world quite unexpectedly.

BBC T.V. "Kelly's point of View"
25 April 1957.

APPENDIX A

Why we started Organic Farming

My entry into farming coincided with the introduction of the new agro-chemicals. Agroxone was the first we used - then a white powder that we scattered over the fields with a fertilizer distributor to control the charlock that always seemed to be present in corn on the chalk. It was marvellous. The charlock started curling up and very soon died and we really believed that we had found the answer. Then it was produced in 40 gallon drums as a dark-coloured liquid and we bought sprayers to apply it. This was even better - more acres per day and a more effective kill. And all this at the time we were receiving a subsidy cheque by every post as feather-bedded farmers! No wonder we really thought Utopia had arrived.

Throughout the 1950s more and more chemical sprays were introduced, and in common with most other farmers we used them - at first to control the easy-to-kill annuals and then, as the sprays became more lethal, to control docks, nettles and thistles. There seemed to be at least half-a-dozen new preparations every year and we all used them as fast as we could buy them. Farming had the weed problem licked!

During the 1960s three apparently unrelated cases of man's interference with nature came to my attention and set me thinking. The first concerned our wild English partridge. On the downs around Upavon we had built up a wonderful stock of these lovely birds. Starting in the shooting season of 1953 with a best day's "bag" of 96.1/2 brace (i.e. 193 birds) we had built up to a record day of 520.1/2 brace in 1960. By 1970 our best day had reduced to 50 brace, and we have never had a good stock since. The build-up in stock coincided with the increase in the use of sprays, and in our ignorance - and, I must admit arrogance. - we said that the sprays didn't harm the partridges. We even went so far as to demonstrate that you could pour spray over a coop full of young partridges without harming them in the least. With hindsight I suppose the early sprays were nowhere near as efficient as the ones developed in the 1960s, which meant that they didn't destroy all the weeds in the cornfields as was the case later. As is now well known, a partridge chick depends on insects for the first three weeks of its life, so, while we were not killing the partridges directly, by destroying the weeds on which the insects lived we were effectively depriving the chicks of their vital food supply. A simple but deadly way of destroying partridges - not directly, but at second remove.

The second case was brought to my notice by Rachel Carson's book "Silent Spring", which traced the death of vast numbers of robins in America to the use of DDT on elm trees. What happened was this. Dutch elm disease became established in parts of America and the Americans, not given to doing things by halves, sprayed every elm tree in sight with DDT. They knew that the disease was carried by the elm-bark beetle, so they thought that if they killed all the beetles the disease wouldn't spread. Simple logic! But nature is not that simple. In due course the leaves fell from the trees and were eaten by the worms. The amount of DDT on the leaves eaten by any one worm was insufficient to kill it, but it concentrated the poison in its body (bio-magnification) so that when the luckless robins ate the worms they soon acquired a fatal dose and died. Again, a case of death at second remove.

And the third case was the Thalidomide tragedy. It is still too clearly remembered for it to be necessary to go into details - suffice it to say that here was a drug that came into use after the usual tests applied to human medicines and that could still have such terrible effects. When the story was made known, largely through the Sunday Times "Insight" team's book "Suffer the Children" (Deutsch 1979), it became apparent that adverse data had been withheld by the manufacturer - data which, if made known to the medical committee responsible for passing the drug for human use, would have eliminated it immediately. So I thought: if a drug can be passed fit for people when it is potentially so dangerous, what may be the effects of the dozens (and there were dozens by then) of new agro-chemicals being used on farms so freely? Can we be sure they are safe? Have the long-term effects of these chemicals been studied? And where is the independent Ministry testing station?

APPENDIX B

Nest and Hatch Records 1954

1. Nests found: 137 on Littlecott and 50 on Upavon (total 187) were known and recorded.
2. Peak first egg periods: April 26th – 28th on Littlecott and April 24th – 26th on Upavon. Early eggs were laid on April 14th, 15th and 16th.
3. Dates of completion of clutch: The peak periods occurred on May 11th and 12th.
4. Clutch size: A total of 2412 eggs were laid in 156 completed nests which gives an average clutch size of 15.5 eggs per nest.
5. % Hatch: From successful nests, an overall average hatch of 96.7% was achieved.
6. Peak hatching period: June 2nd – 4th.
7. Chicks hatched: 1943 chicks were known to have hatched from 127 nests, giving an average of 15.3 per nest.
8. Nest losses: To predators – 18 out of 187 = 9.6%
   Other causes – 38 out of 187 = 20.3%

   Main culprits – rooks, 13 nests, weather, 28 nests
   131 nests out of 187 hatched successfully = 70.05%

APPENDIX C

'Old Boy' News (for our 1991 sale)

Rushall Horses - Known to have evented:

Our name	Now known as	Bought	Points (3.4.91)
Blackthorn of Rushall		1976	63
Catkin of Rushall		1983	207
Charlie Brown IV		Home-bred	364
Dubonnet	Royal Canyon	1981	61
Gulliver	Master Gulliver	1985	71
Grenville		1985	44
Harmony	Welsh Harmony	1985	91
Harlequin of Rushall		1983	30
Hurricane		1986	34

Rushall Horses - Sold abroad

Fargo of Rushall	Germany
Beech	Austria
Cresta	Switzerland
Elwood	Canada
Eskimo	Belgium

Appendix C

<u>Galahad</u>   Denmark
<u>Greylag</u>   Ireland
<u>Dubonnet</u> (Royal Canyon)   Spain
<u>Flamingo</u>   Germany
<u>Innisfree</u>   Sweden

Rushall Stars ! (Since previous sale - 1989)

<u>Fathom</u>   Now known as BOOTLEG   1983 Sale
"Bootleg has always been so very kind in and out of the stable and wonderful to travel, is always the same, so good........We have had all kinds of fun with him....."
Horse and Hound Working Hunter of the Year 1989 and 1990
British Open Hunter Championship – Locko Park 1989 and 1990

<u>Kestrel</u>   Now known as Double Trouble   1987 Sale
'Lovely character and temperament'
1989 4 y.o. Masterlock Champion.
1990 Overall Masterlock Champion.

<u>Harmony</u>   Now Welsh Harmony   1985 Sale
"1990 was a most successful season with him upgrading to Advanced and including 6th. at Windsor 3 DE. We are so pleased with Harry"

<u>Kingfisher</u>   Now known as Impetuous.   1987 Sale
"He has a wonderful temperament.....I think he is the best potential eventer I've ever had."

<u>Jutland</u>   Now known as Red Domino. 1987 Sale

Appendix C

"A wonderful horse with temperament to match. Has been successful at all three disciplines at local level - indeed, is rarely unplaced."

<u>Larkspur</u>					1989 Sale

"Has a fantastic temperament, but is a little cautious."

<u>Monk</u>		Now known as Monkey		1989 Sale

"He has a fantastic temperament and is so easy to handle."

<u>Kandahar</u>		Now known as Young Alfie		1987 Sale

"Has run in three Novice Hurdle Races showing a great deal of promise."

<u>Mayfly</u>					1989 Sale

"A very nice type of horse showing a deal of quality and moves superbly."

<u>Moss</u>					1989 Sale

".....he is a joy to own."

<u>Charlie Brown IV</u>					1981 Sale

Bred at Rushall. Now retired to the hunting field after gaining 364 points in B.H.S. Events with Ian Stark.

<u>Lloyder</u>		Now known as Ancient Heir		1989 Sale

"Charming horse with magnificent temperament. We have great hopes of him."

<u>Legend</u>		Now known as Triscombe		1989 Sale

"He was 8th in his first Pre-Novice - clear round both and inside the time without trying, so we are delighted with him."

Appendix C

<u>Moonraker</u>   1989 Sale

"He is now broken and going very sweetly - moves extremely well and is much loved by all."

APPENDIX D

Odds and ends

For by Agony Column standards, an old Boy is worth two young men.
    Peter Fleming. "Brazilian Adventure".

It requires far less courage to be an explorer than a chartered accountant.
    Peter Fleming. "Brazilian Adventure".

New York. Unnamed officials today stated that anything might happen anytime.
    Daily Express. 27 Jan. 1945.

Definition of Blotting Paper.
The stuff you look for while the ink dries.
    Anon.

News is what a chap who doesn't care much about anything wants to read.
    Evelyn Waugh. "Scoop".

It is water that causes mud, and it is water that removes it.

Appendix D

It is your will that makes you commit sin, and it is by your will alone that you can be purified.
      Hindu poet.   Vemana.

Always have your underclothes nice in case you get run over by a bus.
      Marjorie Sharp."Cluny Brown"

In the year 1943 India was visited by Famine, Pestilence and Beverley Nichols.
      N.G. Jog.   "Judge or Judas?"

But I had lost my curiosity: and when that happens to the Englishman in India it is time for him to leave.
      John Harris.   "Traveller from Tokyo".

Yes, people are always better than their politics.
      Warwick Deeping.   "Sackcloth into Silk".

Deal (England).   Aug. 7th.
"..... *bathers watched in consternation while the 1000 ton U.S. tanker steamed straight for the shore and grounded here today. The embarrassed American skipper explained that he had made a slight mistake in navigation.*"
      The Statesman.   10 August 1946.

India 1947. Buying a mackintosh.
"...... *not Indian, Sahib - waterproof*".
      Mohan Lal.   Roorkee Bazaar. 1947.

Appendix C

The curfew tolls the knell of parting day,
The line of cars winds slowly o'er the lea,
The pedestrian homeward plods his absent-minded way
And leaves this world quite unexpectedly.
        BBC.T.V.   "Kelly's point of View". 25 April 1957.

Shepherd: "The rooks are eating all the sheep grub."
Farmer: "Here's a gun - see what you can do."
              Next day farmer sees dozens of dead rooks and asks Shepherd how he did it.
Shepherd: "I put all the troughs in a line and when the rooks came I let fly into them."
Farmer: "But that wasn't very sporting."
Shepherd: "Oh, yes it was. Before I fired I shouted 'Look out'."

Boss tells his man off for being home early from the fields.
Man: "But I can't understand that -
           I walked home ever so slow."

Jethro, our second grandson then aged four to his father (Nigel) after arriving home from playing in a football match.
        "Did you score a goal, Dad?"
        "No"
        "Why do you always don't?"

ISBN 141208599-3